THE

IMAGE AND NUMBER TREATISE

THE ORACLE AND THE WAR ON FATE

Volume II

RESEARCHES
ON
THE TOLTEC I CHING

WILLIAM DOUGLAS HORDEN

3 + 4 :: 6 + 1 :: RETURN

Back Cover Art

Copyright 2009 Martha Ramirez-Oropeza

DELOK PUBLISHING, ITHACA

ISBN-13:
978-1499587180

ISBN-10:
149958718X

DEDICATION

To The Inner Master Within All

THREE-FOLD KEY
TO TRIGRAM TRANSPOSITION

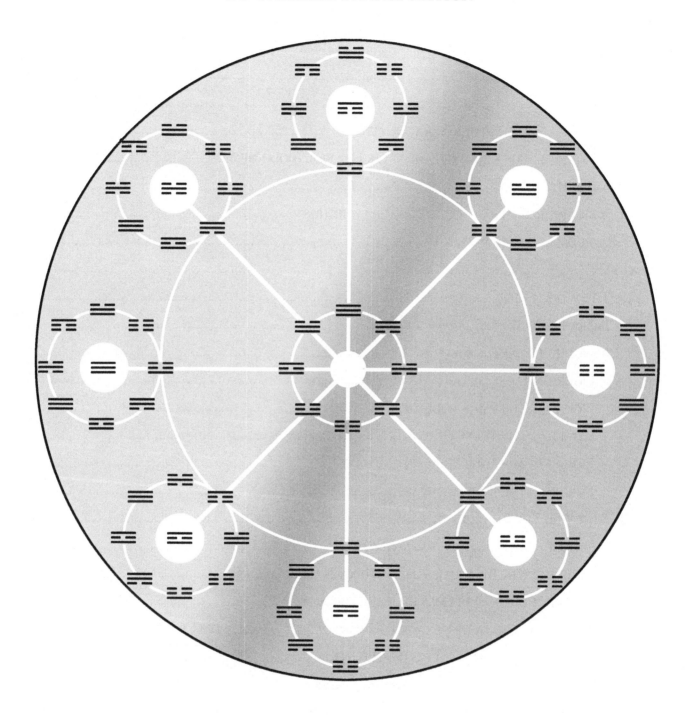

INNERMOST CIRCLE: FU XI, OR BEFORE HEAVEN, ARRANGEMENT

MIDDLE CIRCLE: KING WEN, OR AFTER HEAVEN, ARRANGEMENT

OUTER CIRCLE: TOLTEC I CHING, OR OPEN SECRET, ARRANGEMENT

CONTENTS

INTRODUCTION

This second volume of *Researches On The Toltec I Ching* reinterprets significant portions of the *Ten Wings* classic commentary on the I Ching in light of the transcultural approach of *The Toltec I Ching*. Specifically, it renders the sections known as *Discussion of the Trigrams* and the *Great Treatise* into terms consistent with the mystical-rational methodology of *The Toltec I Ching*. In doing so, it follows the structure laid out in *Book II: The Material* as presented in the Wilhelm/Baynes translation of *The Book of Changes*.

BOOK I: THE ORACLE WHISPERS

CHAPTER I

1. My relationship with human beings began millennia ago. At first, we communicated only through dreams and coincidences and revelatory visions, but with familiarity our spirits harmonized and we devised THE CHANGES so that our exchange could be passed from generation to generation.

Because numbers each have a soul of their own, their transformations into one another reveal the one soul dwelling within every body: Therefore, THE CHANGES are built on the law of number, revealing the invisible path of immortality running like liquid light through the shadowlands of mortality and fate.

So we agreed that the soul of spirit is the number three and that the soul of matter is the number two. From this, the lines were born and the hexagrams formed and the basis of our exchange was established.

My relationship with your spiritual ancestors was based on our harmony with The Way and its law of spiritual cause-and-effect. We witnessed the rise of individual consciousness and the falling away of collective consciousness and we marked that passage with the landmarks of the trigrams. We witnessed the rise of self-interest and the falling away of the common good and we marked that passage with the landmarks of the hexagrams. We witnessed the rise of unquestioned fate and the falling away of unquestioned freedom and we marked that passage with the lines.

COMMENTARY

THE CHANGES is a microcosm of the greater macrocosm of UNIVERSAL CHANGE, which it embodies in the six lines of the 64 hexagrams. The way in which the lines change nature is precisely identical to the way that generative energy, or *qi*, manifests in the physical world. In this opening chapter, the Oracle speaks directly to us, making it clear that THE CHANGES is a direct manifestation of its own inner workings, which is the fundamental harmony of the spiritual cause-and-effect.

Rather than communicate solely through subjective experiences like dreams and synchronicities, the Oracle was concerned enough with the heightened sensitivities of human nature that it entered into a compact with human beings, agreeing to communicate through an objective mechanism that could be used to accumulate wisdom and pass guidance to the succeeding generations. This mechanism whereby the six lines alternate between broken and solid in order to transform hexagrams into one another is what we call THE CHANGES.

Fundamental to THE CHANGES is the soul of each number, which is a direct manifestation of its particular quality of the sacred. The way in which numbers transform through arithmetic calculations reveals their hidden relationships: for those who can name the souls within numbers, a formula like $4 - 2 = 2$ speaks volumes. The calculations among numbers in THE CHANGES allows the diviner to consider all the possible paths at every juncture and choose those that lead to the path of freedom rather than those predetermined by fate.

The Oracle communicates by the law of meaningful coincidence, using the apparently random tossing of coins to build up the hexagrams line-by-line. This ages-old method of consulting the Oracle is known as *The Forest Of Fire Pearls*.

Beginning with the initial assignment of odd numbers to the soul of spirit and even numbers to the soul of matter—and setting aside the number *one* at this juncture because of its all-inclusive nature—the number *three* was assigned to the obverse, or heads, side of a coin and the number *two* to the reverse, or tails, side. Each of the six throws of coins determines the nature of one of the six lines of a hexagram.

Each throw uses three coins, so that four possible results can be obtained for each line:

Three Tails =	$2 + 2 + 2 = 6$
Two Tails & One Heads =	$2 + 2 + 3 = 7$
Two Heads & One Tails =	$3 + 3 + 2 = 8$
Three Heads =	$3 + 3 + 3 = 9$

Being more balanced between both sides of the coins, the totals 7 and 8 were assigned a static nature of solid and broken lines:

$7 = $ ———— $8 = $ —— ——

Being over-balanced on one side of the coins, the totals 6 and 9 were assigned a changing nature of changing broken and changing solid lines:

$$6 = \text{——x——} \qquad\qquad 9 = \text{——o——}$$

Because there are only two types of lines—solid and broken—changing broken lines change into solid lines and vice versa: a six, having come to its extreme, changes into its opposite, a seven and, likewise, a nine, having reached its extreme, changes into its opposite, an eight.

$$\text{——x——} \quad \text{—>} \quad \text{————} \qquad \text{(6 changing to a seven)}$$
$$\text{——o——} \quad \text{—>} \quad \text{—— ——} \qquad \text{(9 changing to an eight)}$$

In this way, the hexagrams were built from the bottom line to the top, creating a symbol representing the present situation and, if changing lines appeared, the way in which developments are trending into a future situation. The souls of the hexagrams carry meanings into the physical and psychological world, which allow the Oracle to answer its questioners.

The Oracle uses this first section of the work to remind us of the degeneration of civilization and the way THE CHANGES adopted meanings and values to steer civilization back on course. THE CHANGES came into being at that juncture of human evolution when the collective co-conscious stage of humanity was developing the individual conscious stage: this passage from Being into Thinking was marked with the emergence of the eight trigrams, which reveal the archetypal states of change from creation to completion. With the rise of individual consciousness came the advent of self-interest, greed and dominance: the way to live harmoniously among social conflict and stress became of the utmost concern, so the hexagrams became repositories of wisdom in the lifelong effort to balance the inner and outer. With the rise of social conditioning came the cultural mores and values that establish routinized thinking and narrowed worldviews: the way to recognize and avoid the herd mentality and a trivialized life became of the utmost concern, so the line changes became the specific means by which the Oracle could point out the path of freedom lying hidden among all the predetermined choices society offers.

2. Together we explored the nature of freedom and fate, uncovering the pattern of birth and death in both the outer world of the seasons and the inner world of human perception. Together we explored the generative energy of qi, uncovering the pattern of movement and resistance in both the outer world of nature and the inner world of human responses. Together we explored the humane and the just, uncovering the pattern of the great civilizing influence at work in both the outer world of society and the inner world of human nature. These three dimensions of human experience we embodied in the three lines of the trigrams and the six lines of the hexagrams.

Together we followed THE CHANGES to its origin, wherein there exists only one hexagram of light and shadow, each of its lines alternating solid and broken, transforming into each of the sixty-four hexagrams in turn, just as the one soul passes among all potential bodies.

COMMENTARY

The words *freedom* and *fate* have very specific meanings for the Oracle. Fate symbolizes the way in which a lifetime follows a predetermined course, which might be set by circumstances of birth and upraising, or by cultural norms and expectations, or by personal habits of thought and feeling, or by the invisible influence of spiritual cause-and-effect. Fate is the trap human nature falls prey to when it abdicates its mandate for self-realization and allows itself, instead, to be molded by the dictates of the times. This is likened to an uncontrolled out-flowing of one's life-force that results in a dissipation of one's core energy, diminished sensitivity to subtle energies beyond the five senses, compulsive striving for recognition and acknowledgement, heightened insecurity and competitiveness, and diminished ability to experience joy, contentment and fulfillment.

Freedom, on the other hand, symbolizes the Other Way, the Backwards Way, the Return Way. It signifies the ability to step out of one's conditioning, to voluntarily set aside the sum of the body's memories and respond to the ever-new moment with an utter lack of inclinations or preconceptions. Freedom is part and parcel of the road of the Oracle, a lifeway that centers on not identifying with anything: it is the expression of a self-discipline that interrupts fate at every turn, cultivating an open heart-mind that does not waste energy.

Where fate trivializes life, freedom ennobles it. Core energy does not run out, it is turned back on itself to replenish and renew and reinvigorate itself. Awareness is heightened to ever-greater degrees of sensitivity to the One. A calm benevolent detachment from the outcome of actions settles over one. A profound trust in the benevolence of the World Soul dispels all doubts and fears. An acceptance of the beauty and loving-kindness of Life kindles a flame of gratitude that slowly grows into the bonfire of the ecstatic life.

Among the hexagrams, the Path of Fate is represented by the predetermined direction and momentum of the sequence from Provoking Change to Safeguarding Life. Contrariwise, the Path of Freedom is represented by the answers of the Oracle, which allow the diviner to leap out of the Path of Fate, moving back and forth within the sequence of change, according to one's responsiveness to the time.

In this vein, the concept of *birth and death* is a symbol of the beginnings and endings of things, the way in which things come into being and return to nonbeing. Diviners cultivate their outer sensitivity to incipient signs of future growth and early signs of future deterioration—and their inner sensitivity to the arising and falling away of each unbidden thought, feeling and memory. Likewise, the patterned distribution of generative energy of *qi* can be observed in the eight archetypes of the trigrams, whose combinations of outer and inner qualities form the sixty-four hexagrams.

Beyond this, there is the Great Mystery, the Great Awakening Spirit, working from both outside and inside each person to bring about a time of peace and prospering for all. With each generation, the fundamentals of humaneness and just treatment of all become more deeply ingrained and more widely accepted. This is the result of the Universal Civilizing Spirit: The inevitable Golden Age of Humanity, which is the full realization and completion of the original Act of Creation.

These three aspects of inner and outer nature, attributed to Spirit, Nature and Humanity, find their expression in the top, bottom and middle lines of the trigrams, respectively—and in the top two, bottom two and middle two lines of the hexagrams, respectively.

Ultimately, the origin of THE CHANGES cannot be found in Thinking—it has to be sought in the depths of Being that exists prior to the advent of language and the division of experience into linearity and duality. In this state of communion, there arises a sudden awareness of the mystical union between diviner and primordial image: all the hexagrams collapse into their single Being, just as all of time is ever collapsing into its single present moment. Devoid of linearity, there is no sequence of sixty-four hexagrams. Devoid of duality, there is no divide between Oracle and diviner. The communion among all things establishes the basis of the divinatory moment: question, thought, intent, coins, answer—the single hexagram manifests in its present guise, just as all the heartbeats of this lifetime manifest in this single present heartbeat.

Chapter II

3. Sun and Moon establish the compass points. Mountain and Lake level the high and the low. Lightning and Wind reinforce one another. Water and Fire are two halves of a mysterious whole.

The outflow of generative energy follows the forward movement into the past. The cultivating of generative energy follows the backward movement into the future. Therefore, THE CHANGES has forward-moving numbers and backward-moving numbers.

<u>Commentary</u>

Here we are introduced to the trigrams proper, first in their nontemporal relationships of paired opposites and then in their developmental phases of cyclic change—

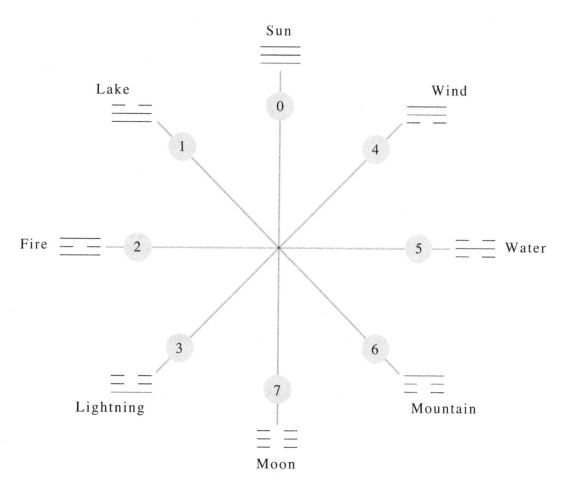

FIGURE 1: THE PRIMAL ARRANGEMENT

As paired opposites, the trigrams complement one another from opposite ends of the four axes: Sun and Moon comprise the vertical axis, while Fire and Water determine the horizontal axis; Lightning and Wind complement each other along one diagonal while Mountain and Lake do so along the other.

When considered as four cosmic forces, the trigrams appear as a perfectly balanced whole, whose equilibrium creates and sustains all of existence *in potential*. In their perfectly balanced state, there are no dynamics to reach into the manifested world: they create and sustain all existence by holding in potential the empty vessel within which all of space and time and life can exist.

Below are the eight trigram pairs *Sun-Moon*, *Lightning-Wind*, *Water-Fire*, and *Mountain-Lake* with their representative icons:

When the trigrams move, however, they stir up the archetypal forces and set them in a cyclic progression from creation to completion. Starting with Sun, the cycle moves counter-clockwise to Lake and Fire and Lightning, at which point it pivots across its axis to Wind and then descends clockwise to Water and Mountain and Moon—whereupon it pivots again across the vertical axis to Sun and begins the entire cycle over again (see Figure 1).

0	1	2	3	4	5	6	7

When the generative energy moves along this forward-moving cycle, then it materializes within the physical world, accounting for all the phenomena in the universe, including the human body. Because this *cycle of existence* is what develops all things from birth to death, it carries everything into the past. This is the cycle of forward-moving numbers.

When practitioners reverse this flow of generative energy—taking it from Moon to Mountain to Water to Wind and then across to Lightning to Fire to Lake and then Sun—they take up the great work of the ancients' undertaking to return the Many to the One. Because this *cycle of essence* establishes the time-bound destiny of each thing within its timeless origin, it carries everything into the future. This is the cycle of backward-moving numbers.

Figure 1 is a living relic of a sacred technology of great antiquity traditionally attributed to the culture hero, Fu Xi, of ancient China. It is also called the *Before Heaven* arrangement.

> 4. *Lightning spurs, Wind unblocks, Water soaks, Fire shows, Mountain calms, Lake excites, the Sun empowers, the Moon provides.*

Commentary

Here we are apprised of the essential nature of each of the eight trigrams as they are paired in equipoise in the Primal Arrangement.

Lightning inspires and motivates, spurring things to change, often through unexpected and surprising developments. Wind is a persistent, patient influence that makes its way through obstacles the way the wind enters through the cracks in a wall or the roots of a tree slowly opens up stone. Water signifies the kind of unpredictable change that immerses things within it, entering into them and carrying them along, like a river rushing through a gorge or cloth taking dye. Fire signifies the kind of change that illuminates the hidden, bringing to view both profound understanding and shallow opinion. Mountain is a stabilizing force that brings things to rest and easy quiet, the way a thousand-foot cliff presents the traveler with a stopping-place. Lake brings happiness and companionship, the way water draws all beings together peacefully in times of thirst. Sun kindles the little sun within the individual, awakening the kind of strength and flexibility that makes great feats possible. Moon is the great mother of the sea, the womb of fertility, the treasure house of resources in which things are completed and perfected.

5. The one soul emerges in the sign of Lightning. It develops in the sign of Wind. It recognizes in the sign of Fire. It shares in the sign of the Moon. It welcomes in the sign of Lake. It triumphs in the sign of the Sun. It bears in the sign of Water. It polishes in the sign of Mountain.

Commentary

Here we are given the meanings of the trigrams in the arrangement traditionally attributed to King Wen of the Chou dynasty. It envisions change as cyclic, beginning with Lightning and moving clockwise to end at Mountain before it starts again.

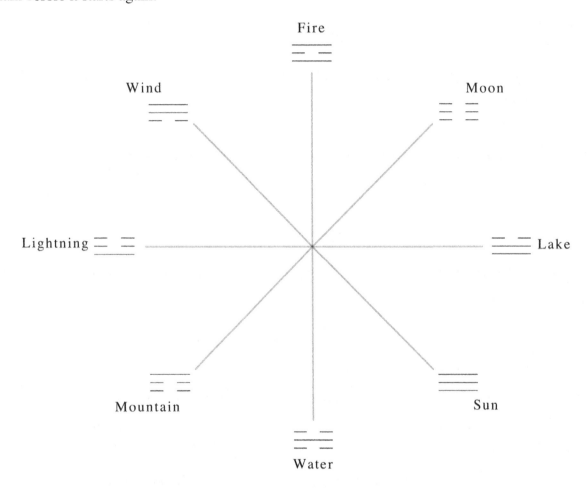

FIGURE 2: THE KING WEN, OR AFTER HEAVEN, ARRANGEMENT

Just as we are seldom aware of being on a globe spinning on its axis in the void of space, our social conditioning numbs us to the fact that all is one living soul that moves within and among all things. Insofar as it is ensouled in this living planet, it is called the World Soul. Insofar as it is ensouled in living beings, it is called spirit. Insofar as it is ensouled in the whole of living creation, it is called the One.

20

To those sensitive to the One, it is apparent that spirit enters the world sudden as Lightning and is shaped by the persistent influence of Wind. As it matures, it discerns both sameness and difference in the light of Fire, so that no benefit is held back in the phases of Moon. It meets all with the open heart of Lake and so succeeds through the inner power of Sun. As its accomplishments unfold, it endures the passage of its works through the straights of fate in Water and achieves mastery of substance in the timelessness of Mountain.

This is the natural birthright of every person, the natural course of coming into and going out of: it can, unfortunately, be interrupted by circumstances of birth, upbringing and culture. In such cases, Lightning can present as trauma, Wind as susceptibility, Fire as convention, Moon as exploitation, Lake as naiveté, Sun as dominance, Water as grief, and Mountain as a dead end. THE CHANGES is not an anachronistic work of timeworn ideas—it is the living soul of *freedom in every sense*, seeking expression through each individual's process of self-realization. The Oracle's intent is primarily to describe the spiritual landscape and orient the inner compass to the true pole. Only secondarily is it concerned with avoiding obstacles and remedying unease. This is because those who can turn their backs all at once on circumstances of birth, upbringing and culture plunge directly into the natural course of metamorphosis.

6. *The one soul circulates among all things and acts through them. Of the generative energy that awakens things, Lightning is the most potent. Of the generative energy that influences things, Wind is the most potent. Of the generative energy that grasps things, Fire is the most potent. Of the generative energy that completes things, the Moon is the most potent. Of the generative energy that heartens things, Lake is the most potent. Of the generative energy that begets things, the Sun is the most potent. Of the generative energy that fills things, Water is the most potent. Of the generative energy that reunites things, Mountain is the most potent.*

Such is the Open Secret of the world: Everything contains its own contradiction. Lightning and Wind are two halves of the same atmosphere. Water and Fire are two halves of the same vapor. Mountain and Lake are two halves of the same landscape. Only by harmonizing the duality within things can generative energy be used to change things so that they more perfectly reflect the intent of the one soul.

Commentary

Beneath the surface of the senses, standing prior to material form, there is generative energy. This energy, which translates the ethereal intent of the one soul into physical manifestation, has been called *qi* since ancient times in China. In Section 6, above, we see that this generative energy is a true mediating force between the physical and non-physical: each of the eight archetypal elements of change is shown here to manifest in both its function in form and its function in perception—both, in other words, as that which is perceived and that which perceives.

Lightning awakens things in the world but it is also the sense organ that can perceive awakenings. Wind influences things in the world but it is also the sense organ that can perceive influence. Fire grasps things in the world but it is also the sense organ that can perceive understanding. Moon completes things in the world but it is also the sense organ that can perceive completion. Lake heartens things in the world but it is also the sense organ that can perceive heartening. Sun begets things in the world but it is also the sense organ that can perceive creation. Water fills things in the world but it is also the sense organ that can perceive filling. Mountain reunites things in the world but it is also the sense organ that can perceive reuniting.

The eight forces of change, in this way, are the senses of the world and human nature, both. It is the same generative energy that manifests as material form *and* the sense organs that perceive form. Between nature and human nature, generative energy flows in its capacity as the universal pattern of perception: the world perceives spirit and adapts to fit it, just as spirit perceives the world and adapts to fit it. It is this *mutual sensing and complementing* that co-creates the material universe as a mirror of the underlying harmony of the spiritual universe.

This section concludes by reverting to the pairing of opposing forces presented in the Primal Arrangement in order to reinforce the importance of the unity within duality. Lightning and Wind are seen here as the sudden and gradual forces at work in the psychological environment within which we dwell, where Lightning changes things from without, while Wind changes things from within. The vapor of which Fire and Water comprise complementary halves is the steam produced by their union—and so, the mists of the land and the breath of the body when hot and cold air meet. As the living breath of both the world and the body, this vapor has long been the symbol of the generative energy that animates all matter and brings it all to conscious awareness eventually.

Fire, in this sense, represents the known, whereas Water represents the unknown. As such, their vapor symbolizes the cooking pot, the sustenance of life-giving nourishment that stands midway between the atmosphere of the sky and the landscape of the world. Mountain and Lake, then, are the high and low places of the material and social world in which we dwell, where Mountain speaks of difficulty and aloneness, while Lake speaks of ease and companionship. The Great Work of perfecting human nature in order to bring it into accord with already-perfected nature and spirit depends on balancing and harmonizing these primal polarities in practical concentrations of intention that bring about beneficial change for all.

Chapter III

7. The Sun is daring. The Moon is caring. Lightning is surprising. Wind is improvising. Water is confusing. Fire is choosing. Mountain is waiting. Lake is elating.

Commentary

Again, the eight trigrams are arranged according to their paired opposites, this time in a rhymed scheme to aid in memorization. Because Sun is strong and creative, it expresses *daring* in the way it begins things. Because Moon is nurturing and fulfilling, it expresses *caring* in the way it completes things. Because Lightning is sudden and unexpected, it expresses *surprising* in the way it enlivens things. Because Wind is changeable and accommodating, it expresses *improvising* in the way it resolves things. Because Water is deep and dark, it expresses *confusing* in the way it overwhelms things. Because Fire is clarifying and discerning, it expresses *choosing* in the way it decides things. Because Mountain is quiet and unmoving, it expresses *waiting* in the way it stills things. Because Lake is rejoicing and welcoming, it expresses *elating* in the way it ennobles things.

8. The Sun is controversial without and adventurous within. The Moon is fulfilled without and encouraging within. Lightning is tested without and resolute within. Wind is tempered without and inquisitive within. Water is insecure without and indecisive within. Fire is secure without and decisive within. Mountain is obstructed without and reserved within. Lake is accepted without and appreciative within.

Commentary

The characteristics of the trigrams are developed further here, with a particular emphasis on the part they play in their respective hexagrams. What is called "without" refers to the upper trigram of a hexagram and by "within" is meant the lower trigram of a hexagram. From this, we can see that the nature of a trigram is differs subtlety depending on whether it constitutes the upper or lower trigram of hexagram. This is because each hexagram is considered a situation comprised of an inner nature and outer circumstances.

Depending on the context of the question, an individual's inner nature might signify their personality or values or goals, while the outer nature might represent their relationship or workplace or current events. Likewise, a nation's lower trigram might point to its domestic state while the outer trigram points to its foreign relations.

It is in this sense that each hexagram is considered a *situation comprised of an inner and outer nature*. And it is for this reason that each trigram carries a slightly different meaning depending on whether it occupies the upper or lower position of its hexagram. Sun, for example, is often interpreted as controversial in its external interactions while from within, it expresses itself as adventurous. Understanding the way the lower and upper trigrams merge to create the meaning of the hexagram contributes materially to arriving at a deeper interpretation of the overall situation arising from the commingling of its inner and outer natures.

> *9. The Sun is creation, the Moon is completion. Lightning is motivation, Wind is adaptation. Water is mystery, Fire is understanding. Mountain is stillness, Lake is wonder.*

Commentary

Utilizing the paired opposites of the Primal Arrangement, we are given here the set of the most general and most often-used characteristics for the trigrams. When the trigrams are viewed in their developmental phases of cyclic change, we can see their progression from Creation to Wonder to Understanding to Motivation to Adaptation to Mystery to Stillness to Completion. In this order of completeness lies the open secret of bringing forth beneficial endeavors and securing good fortune.

From Creation to Completion is but a single moment between the radiance and reflecting of light. Uniting Motivation and Adaptation fuses undaunted strength of purpose with utmost flexibility to changing conditions. Exploring the depths of Mystery leads to deeper Understanding, just as exploring the depths of Understanding leads to deeper Mystery. Without Stillness, Wonder carries the soul away—just as without Wonder, Stillness numbs and paralyzes the soul.

> *10. The Sun is the masculine half, the Moon is the feminine half. Lightning is the masculine half, Wind is the feminine half. Water is the masculine half, Fire is the feminine half. Mountain is the masculine half, Lake is the feminine half.*

<u>Commentary</u>

Within the four pairs of opposing forces of change, there is a masculine and feminine half. This ancient formulation of the trigrams was developed long ago into a set of familial relationships wherein Sun and Moon are thought of as the father and mother of the other six trigrams. Lightning and Wind, then, represent the eldest son and eldest daughter, while Water and Fire signify the middle son and middle daughter, and Mountain and Lake denote the youngest son and youngest daughter.

11. The Sun is spirit, the animating power of the seed, the creative impulse to fashion life in new and more meaningful ways. Its principal manifestation is direct purposeful action toward a goal. It can signify arrogance or too strong an approach to matters, not taking the concerns of others into account. Can also signify self-righteous attitude, a sense of being right and overly condemning of others. Loves to start new things, not always dedicated to seeing them through to completion.

The Moon is nature, the perfect reflection of spirit, the loving-kindness of the world that pours the benefit of air, water, food, and light onto all without preference. Its principal manifestation is indirect action seeking to establish alliances based on shared concerns. It can signify too much compliance with the will of others, an overabundance of compassion with a deficit of wisdom. Effortless contentment and productive fulfillment. Loves the sacredness of everyday rituals that give activities meaning.

Lightning is the sudden emergence of the unforeseen. It startles and agitates things into motion. As lightning, its brightness is exceeded only by the sun. As thunder, only silence is more deafening. It stirs things up when a new equilibrium is needed. It can signify a willingness to resort to force or pressure, a strong will able to intimidate. Can also signify the kind of trauma that leaves a deep scar in the memory. The force of will that accomplishes goals. The ability to surprise oneself as well as others. A sudden unexpected turn of events. Loves incongruities and meaningful coincidences.

Wind is patient effort directed toward a goal, a sustained subtle pressure to change something. It is tireless and unrelenting exertion to overcome obstacles and make inroads against opposition. It can signify manipulation, influence by insinuation into another's sphere. It can also signify an unwillingness to change goals or direction. Success by adapting to changing situations. Gradual development that attains its highest aspiration. Loves to move between things.

Water is mystery, the unknowable and uncertain course of good fortune. It is the danger of too much or too little, the importance of seeking modesty and benevolence. It is the risk of setting forth intentions that may clash with those of others. It is the gamble of an endeavor or undertaking. It is the part of the situation or other person we do not know about. It is the unseen forces at work around us. It is the difficulty of making a decision without enough information. Loves filling up empty places.

Fire is personal knowledge, subjective understanding. It is clarity of mind and the ability to view matters from multiple points of view. It is understanding others as well as oneself. It is personal experience and the wisdom it produces. It can signify short-sighted opinion and one-sided beliefs, an overreliance on what others think and say. Can also signify convictions unsupported by first-hand knowledge. Moving forward confident of one's knowledge and ability. Loves learning.

Mountain is the ability to wait, staying alert yet relaxed. It is immovable because it does not occupy a place. It cannot be exploited because it serves no purpose. It consolidates and stabilizes attention. Its action takes the form of doing nothing. It builds up one's reserves. It can signify frustration at being obstructed, a hiatus when forward progress threatens to stall out. Can also signify procrastination and the stagnation that comes with too much introversion. It represents a period of calm isolation in which to prepare for what comes next. Loves peace and tranquility.

Lake is spontaneous enjoyment, shared happiness, resolved tension. It is appreciation and gratitude. It is closeness and familiarity and unconditional acceptance. It is laughter and pleasure, the enjoyment of life. It can signify over-indulging the senses, succumbing to self-defeating forms of gratification. Can also signify the superficiality that comes from an excess of extraversion. It thrives in an immersion of the unity of all things. The ecstatic life. Devotional attitude seeking communion with nature, people and the divine.

Commentary

The trigrammic attributes detailed in Section 11 above can be summarized in Figure 3 below—

Sun Heaven	☰	☀	CREATE	The Impulse that Begins new things. The Source of Starting Anew. Seed of potential. *Create or Perish*
Moon Earth	☷	☾	COMPLETE	Nurturing Power to bring all things to Fruition. The realization of potential. Fulfillment. The midwife bringing all births into being. *Nourish Everything that Touches You*
Lightning Thunder	☳	⚡	SURPRISE	The Unexpected, often a pleasant surprise but sometimes bringing trauma and distress. Sets in motion light. Breakthrough. *Surprise Yourself and Others*
Wind Roots	☴	☁	ADAPT	Persistent energy penetrating the impasses. Discovery. Continuity. Communication. Accommodation. *Flow Around every Obstacle*
Water Ravine	☵	💧	RISK	May be beneficial and nourishing as rain but also has danger of flood or drought. The Unknown. Uncertainty. Risk. Secret. *Make the Unknown Your Home*
Fire Light	☲	🔥	LEARN	Knowledge based on opinion or convention vs understanding and wisdom. Reason. Analysis. Certainty. Attachment. *Learning is Remembering*
Mountain Peak	☶	⛰	STABILIZE	Interruption. Stopping. A Time of Rest. Consolidation and Preparation for next stage. Tranquil Contemplation. *The Center is within You*
Lake Wetland	☱	〜	WONDER	Joyous Gathering Together. Encouraging. Sharing Blessings. Awe in face of creation. Mystic. *Follow Your Curiosity*

FIGURE 3: SUMMARY OF TRIGRAM ATTRIBUTES

BOOK II: FREEDOM AND FATE WITHIN THE CHANGES

PART I

A. THE WORLD VIEW

Chapter I. *The Way of Change*

1. Spirit is not greater, Nature is not lesser—thus we know their essential equality within the unity of the One. Spirit is the invisible half of Nature, just as Nature is the visible half of Spirit—thus we know the sacredness of every change.

Form and Formless appear before us, obeying the law of spiritual cause-and-effect: Generative energy emerges and submerges like the waves of an ocean, leaving solid and broken lines in its wake.

Intentions marshal generative energy into patterns of change: Trends appear before us like the wind sweeping the land in front of the rain. Form and Formless follow the patterns of change: Action and intention are the nature and spirit of good fortune and misfortune. In Spirit, intentions produce Formless actions, just as in Nature, actions produce intentions with Form. From this standpoint we can dwell beside the gate of change, tracing what is coming and going at its headwaters.

Commentary

The lifeway of THE CHANGES is rooted in oneness. The senses of the human body cannot perceive the universe in its entirety—rather, they filter out all the sensory experience that the genetic code has deemed unnecessary for physical survival. The human body is predisposed from within and trained by culture from without to draw just those distinctions between itself and other things that promise greater advantage in its perceived struggle against death. While this has resulted in great success for the human species on the physical level, its essential weakness as a long-range strategy has long been apparent to our ancestors.

The separation of the individual from the Whole can only be experienced if the miraculous grandeur of every aspect of the Whole is not experienced—if oneness, in other words, is not consciously experienced. This unitary experience is repressed in most modern cultures since it explodes the myth of separation, the side-effect of which is an initial collapse of the individual sense of personal self or identity.

It is at this point that the former individual becomes what has been called a *real person*, often pictured as an upside-down person whose experience of being in the Whole is so diametrically opposed to his or her previous experience. This new identity, based upon one's harmonious relationship to all things within the Whole, constitutes a complete shift of attention and intention, away from personal benefit and toward universal benefit.

The lifeway of THE CHANGES, therefore, does not hold Spirit and Nature apart nor does it raise one above the other in importance. That Nature *is* Spirit in the same way that one's own body and spirit are coexistent becomes self-evident to *real persons* and forms the basis of their experience of the miraculous grandeur of the living, metamorphic universe. It is in this sense, then, that every change is vested with a sacred charge to advance, in its own way, the perfection of the Whole.

The universe of Nature and Spirit, of Form and Formless, is mirrored in the broken and solid lines of THE CHANGES, which provide a symbolic map of the way the law of intention distributes formless generative energy into material form. THE CHANGES is a lifeway that sets our feet firmly on the path of universal benefit by making clear how intentions are inner actions that pass out of us, enter the universal field of intentions, and combine with other intentions. Within this field, intentions combine in patterns of action-and-backlash, reflecting decisions that establish the direction and momentum of change: it is this lifeway of stepping back into the universal field of intentions that permits us to sense the unfolding direction and momentum of change, which allows us to predict the nature and course of change so that we might encourage benefit and answer need.

2. The generative energy circulates through the eight trigrams like compass directions and seasons, causing the solid and broken lines to replace one another.

<u>Commentary</u>

The natural order of change is, at every level, the alternation of two complementary poles of change. The unchanging way in which they take each other's place generates the constant unfolding of new potential from the already-realized. This is the reason that THE CHANGES is a symbolic map of every landscape of change: at every level, the archetypal alternation of poles of change produces the same pattern of order and chance.

> *3. Things rejoice in the light of awareness, they stand transfixed in awe in face of the mystery. Understanding provokes metamorphosis, the unknown calls forth adaptation.*

<u>Commentary</u>

Here we return to the Primal Arrangement (also known as the Before Heaven Arrangement) and consider the pattern of order and chance through its counter-clockwise movement among the trigrams —

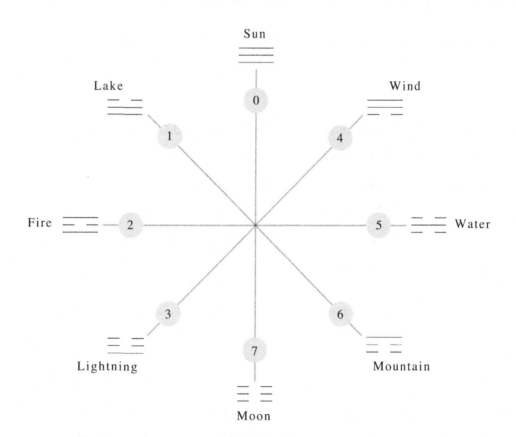

This is an ancient formula that pairs opposing trigrams on the diagonal axes as they depict the lifeway of THE CHANGES—first in their role of sensing and then in their role as responding.

The sequence of sensing runs from Lake (rejoice) to Fire (light of awareness) and then across the axis to Mountain (stand transfixed) and then Water (awe in face of the mystery). Likewise, the sequence of responding runs from Fire (understanding) to Lightning (provokes metamorphosis) and then across the axis to Water (the unknown) and then to Wind (adaptation).

4. Yang generative energy gives rise to the masculine half. Yin generative energy gives rise to the feminine half.

Commentary

No entity is made up entirely of one pole of change. All things are an amalgam of the great Duality of creative forces that make up the unitary nature of the One. In this sense, everything has a masculine and a feminine half, symbolizing the creating and perfecting forces, respectively.

5. The Sun initiates beginnings. The Moon brings them to completion.

Commentary

Where Section 3, above, details the interactions of the six derived trigrams—the so-called three sons and three daughters—this and the following Section detail the respective roles of the so-called parent trigrams. The creative power of the Sun expresses itself in the act of bringing new things into being. The creative power of the Moon expresses itself in the act of nurturing things to fulfillment. The sacred beginning and ending of things is, of course, the context within which the sequence of sensing and the sequence of responding, detailed in Section 3, occur.

6. The Sun does not strive for greatness. The Moon does not contrive to guide things.

Commentary

The action of the creative forces is natural and spontaneous, free of conscious effort. The Sun is not great because of its power to create—it creates because of the greatness of its nature. The Moon does not guide things because of its power to fulfill things—it fulfills things because it is its nature to nurture them.

The *creative intent* of Sun and Moon is to make possible the awakening and self-realization of awareness within every form.

> *7. Each stream has its own course on the way back to the sea. Those who depart from their natural course find themselves alone and without true allies. Those who follow their natural course accord with the One, bringing forth their lifework and finding lifelong allies. Bringing forth works plants seeds of intent in the field of infinity, holding together with true allies cultivates those seeds throughout the field of eternity.*

Commentary

Naturalness of purpose is not, of course, confined to the activity of the creative forces — it is our own ability to reflect that same quality of uncontrived spontaneity that carries us along with the unitary intent of the One. Aligning our own intent to that of the One, we find ourselves in accord with the intents of like-minded souls. This attunement of intent allows us to find companions to share this lifetime with in mutual support of one another's creative intent. This is but one level at which benefiting the Whole benefits oneself.

> *8. When the natural course of return is followed, every step of the journey feels like home. When one is no longer a stranger anywhere, then true Intimacy has been reached and the Universal Civilizing Spirit works out in the open.*

Commentary

This expresses the lifeway of the *return to the act of creation*. Just as the One is the origin of all things, it is their destination. Just as the One is nowhere absent, both origin and destination are immediately present. Just as a drop of water dissolves back into the sea, individual awareness spreads throughout the One.

The lifeway of THE CHANGES is rooted in oneness. It is embodied in individuals, passing through the generations, constant in its eternal purpose of offering to each the opportunity to play an instrumental role in the founding and sustaining of the Golden Age of Humanity.

Until peace and prospering for all has been achieved, civilization will not have attained the first stage of development, thus confining the collective transmutation of human nature to that vanguard of individuals able to transcend their conditioning through their own effort.

1. The spiritual ancestors sensed the world through the eyes of generative energy and devised the hexagrams so that the patterns of change would be perceptible to the following generations. They attached their interpretations in order to point out the roads of fate and freedom.

Commentary

The spiritual ancestors are the great-souled ones throughout history whose lifework was dedicated to embodying the *Universal Civilizing Spirit*. They are those who transcended culture and conditioning to inspire future generations with their generosity of spirit, mind and heart. They are those who call to us to join them—and those we can call on for understanding and wisdom. Moreover, they are the savants, sages, shamans, diviners, and adepts who pierced their own bubble of encapsulation and entered the *world-as-it-is*. This *entering-into*, their collective experience demonstrates, is a voluntary act of surrendering the sense of separation which, in turn, awakens new sensory organs attuned to the flow and distribution of generative energy.

Upon discovering the true forces at work in the materialization of the universe, the ancestors fashioned a way to symbolize the pattern of change that ebbs and flows constantly beneath the threshold of the five senses. As symbols of the creative powers *in action prior to their emergence in material form*, the hexagrams sensitized the following generations to the invisible world of generative energy and, therefore, to coming changes before they breached the surface of appearances. Such is the predictive character of the hexagrams, which trace future changes before their trends appear in the present.

The interpretations of the hexagrams are based upon the 64 possible interactions of the 8 upper trigrams and the 8 lower trigrams. Although as a whole the 64 hexagrams present a single philosophy of life, the interpretation of individual hexagrams varies widely because they extend throughout the entire range of human experience. The *appended interpretations* referred to in this section indicate the entire text accompanying the hexagrams: each points out the *road of fate* by describing the hexagram's situation and dynamics as a whole—and points out the *road of freedom* by describing the best course of action to take in response to the situation.

2. The solid and broken lines take turns filling the six places of the hexagrams: In this way they show how matters once dormant now come to the fore, while matters once important now go unnoticed.

<u>Commentary</u>

The solid lines signify issues that are in the forefront of attention. Broken lines signify issues that are in the background of attention. As explained in the commentary to *Book One, Chapter One*, above, a solid line that is not changing is represented by the number 7, while a broken line that is not changing is represented by the number 8. These represent the stable elements within the hexagram that seek to maintain the status quo.

The line changes within a hexagram, however, represent the dynamic forces at work seeking to establish a new equilibrium by redistributing the issues occupying attention. A changing solid line signifies issues that have been in the forefront of attention but are submerging into the background. A changing broken line, on the other hand, signifies issues that have been in the background of attention and are emerging into the foreground of attention. As explained in the commentary to *Book One, Chapter One*, above, a changing solid line is represented by the number 9, while a changing broken line is represented by the number 6.

The *six places of the hexagrams* referred to in this section indicates the six lines of each hexagram that, read from the bottom, up, represent the archetypal issues within each situation.

Top Line:	Disengagement, Interdependence
Fifth Line:	Authority, Empowerment
Fourth Line:	Responsibility, Independence
Third Line:	Separation, Alienation
Second Line:	Trust, Attachment
Bottom Line:	Vulnerability, Dependence

3. The window of opportunity opens and closes, bestowing good fortune and misfortune in accord with the law of spiritual cause-and-effect: What shame is there in benefiting others, what dishonor is there in treating everything as sacred? Just as a great mountain creates its own weather, constancy of intention and action creates its own future.

Commentary

Here the Oracle reminds us of the importance of timing and steadfastness. Timing is essential in recognizing when to act and when to wait: this requires a sense of the flow of events across the terrain just ahead—and the mobility and versatility to arrive at the juncture of opportunities neither too early nor too late.. Steadfastness is essential in holding to the principles of *universal benefit* and *universal sacredness* in our moment-to-moment actions and intentions—the incremental accumulation of such concentrated purposefulness creates a prow wake of generative energy ahead of us that aligns us with constructive forces of like kind.

4. Changing lines trace the paths of fate and freedom. Solid and broken lines trace the masculine and feminine halves as they occupy the six stages of the hexagrams. As the lines move, they trace the shifting relationships between Nature, Spirit, and Humanity.

Commentary

Here the line changes are shown in relationship to fate and freedom: the interpretation of each line change describes its place in the situation as a whole (fate) and the best response to events (freedom). Knowing when to end things, how to stop things, how to withdraw from matters in the right way—all these are as important as knowing how to start things, how to renew things and how to move on to new things.

Solid lines symbolize *direct purposeful action* (masculine half) and broken lines symbolize *unconditional heartfelt nurturing* (feminine half). In this sense, the masculine half of each person is thought of as a fire element willing to tunnel through a mountain to reach its goal, while the feminine half of each person is thought of as a water element flowing around the mountain but its goal is to nourish everything it touches along the way. This worldview gives rise to a philosophy of *need* (illnesses) and *benefit* (medicines)—

ILLNESSES

FALSE FIRE (NEGATIVE MASCULINE)	FALSE WATER (NEGATIVE FEMININE)
Irritation Frustration Stubbornness Anger Hostility Aggression Violence	Stagnation Apathy Indecisiveness Self-Pity Resentment Depression Despair
(Medicine is *not* "more fire")	(Medicine is *not* "more water")

MEDICINES

TRUE WATER (POSITIVE FEMININE)	TRUE FIRE (POSITIVE MASCULINE)
Medicine for False Fire: *Selfless Service*	Medicine for False Water: *Daring Accomplishment*
Like a river, flexible and adapting, flowing around obstacles	Like tunneling through a mountain to get to the sea
Nurtures everything it touches as it flows to the sea	Direct action toward a goal
Spontaneous. Relationship-driven.	Decisive. Purpose-driven.
OUTER FLEXIBILITY	INNER STRENGTH

FIGURE 4: ILLNESSES AND MEDICINES

—a worldview that seeks to balance the feminine and masculine halves within each person, encouraging an equilibrium based upon the alternation of each half leading the response according to circumstances, as reflected in the six lines of the hexagram: the masculine half may be the best response in the bottom line of vulnerability and the feminine half the best response in the second line of trust, and so on, depending on the specific hexagram.

This section also directs our attention to another way of interpreting the hexagrams and their changes—that of analyzing the so-called *bigrams*.

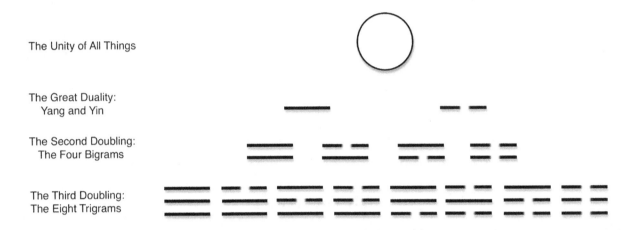

FIGURE 5: THE EMANATIONS OF CREATION

Figure 5, above, depicts the way in which the One gives rise to the Many. Through a series of *doublings*, the infinite and eternal One begets the Two creative forces, which beget the Four seasons of change, which in turn beget the Eight forces of change: the ineffable One begets the Two *lines*, which beget the Four *bigrams*, which in turn beget the Eight *trigrams*.

When this section states, *As the lines move, they trace the shifting relationships between Nature, Spirit, and Humanity*, it refers to the tradition of viewing the hexagrams as *three sets of bigrams* overlaid on the more general interpretation of two sets of trigrams. From this standpoint, the top two lines form the bigram symbolizing Spirit, while the middle two lines form the bigram symbolizing Humanity and the bottom two lines form the bigram symbolizing Nature. This view of the hexagrams provides a way of interpreting the relationships between the divine, the human and the material realms at any particular juncture of time.

TOP LINE FIFTH LINE	SPIRIT
FOURTH LINE THIRD LINE	HUMANITY
SECOND LINE BOTTOM LINE	NATURE

FIGURE 6: THE THREE DIMENSIONS

The four bigrams themselves are conceived of as the cyclic risings and fallings of generative energy that manifest as the seasons of the year. They are identical in nature to the four possible broken and solid lines designated by the numbers 6, 7, 8, and 9. When overlaid on the model of upper and lower trigrams, it is apparent that Humanity's spiritual half (fourth line) comes from Spirit and physical half (third line) from Nature.

As Figure 7, below, shows, the four possible combinations of two lines (the bigrams) *are* the four types of lines in a hexagram (unchanging solid, unchanging broken, changing solid, and changing broken)—

�break break	6	—x—
break solid	7	———
solid break	8	— —
solid solid	9	—⊖—

FIGURE 7: THE FOUR SEASONS OF CHANGE

These four are called the *seasons of change* because they represent the cyclical way that generative energy waxes and wanes in the three dimensions of Spirit, Humanity and Nature. As everything we know about Spirit we have learned by analog from Nature, we can most readily describe this fourfold cycle of waxing and waning in terms of the way in which it manifests in the yearly cycle of renewal, growth, production, decay, and renewal again.

As Figure 8, below, illustrates, this waxing and waning is perceived as a *young light* that arises in Spring, grows to its extreme as the *old light* of Summer, reverses itself as the *young dark* of Autumn, grows to its extreme as the *old dark* of Winter, and reverses again to return as the *young light* of Spring—

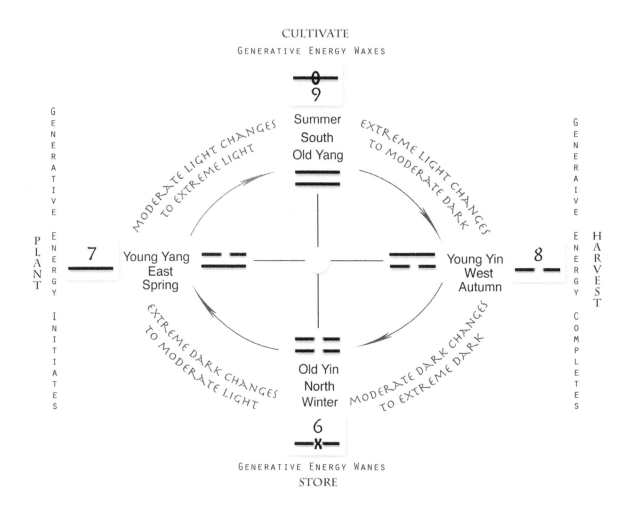

FIGURE 8: THE INNER COMPASS

Generative energy is thought of as *young* and *old* because it is living. It is thought of as *light* and *dark* because the living world is light and warm for the first half of the year and dark and cold for the second half. Because the sun rises in the East at dawn, the *young light* of the unchanging solid line (7) is identical to the initiating energy of Spring. Because the sun reaches its full strength in the South at noon, the *old light* of the changing solid line (9) is identical to the cultivating energy of Summer. Because the sun sets in the West at dusk, the *young dark* of the unchanging broken line (8) is identical to the completing energy of Autumn. And, because the sun disappears in the North at midnight, the *old dark* of the changing broken line (6) is identical to the conserving energy of Winter.

Figure 8 is named *The Inner Compass* because it spatializes time, bringing the seasons and times of day into accord with the compass points. Because everything we know of Humanity we have learned by analog from Nature and Spirit, the inner compass orients us to the waxing and waning energies of body, mind and soul. The materialization of Spirit in Nature manifests most perfectly and completely in the dual Being of Humanity, so that we are most in harmony with the flow of events when our actions are oriented to the cycle of creation and completion—this means attuning ourselves to the time and responding accordingly. The cycle of creation and completion plays itself out on every level which, in the case of human nature, expresses itself in the course of *planting* or sowing seeds of new beginnings in a time of Spring, *cultivating* or developing the growth of things in a time of Summer, *harvesting* or enjoying the fruition of things in a time of Autumn, and *storing* or conserving things in order to rest in a time of Winter. The complexity of human nature requires a sensitivity to the different seasons we occupy at any given moment. For example, we may be enjoying a Spring in one relationship even as we agonize over the Winter of another, meanwhile seeing Autumn arrive in the arena of our vocation even as our spiritual aspirations enter a time of Summer.

The top two lines of any hexagram is occupied by one of the four bigrams, as is the middle and bottom two lines. Just as the union of 8 upper trigrams and 8 lower trigrams produces the 64 possible hexagrams, this set of 4 x 4 x 4 permutations of the bigrams produces the 64 possible hexagrams. This method of interpretation can be used to understand the timing of change within the situation.

—— ——	6	
—— ——	WINTER	SPIRIT
————————	8	
—— ——	AUTUMN	HUMANITY
—— ——	7	
————————	SPRING	NATURE

BIGRAMS OF HEXAGRAM 1 *PROVOKING CHANGE*

As the example above illustrates, the first hexagram, *Provoking Change*, is not just comprised of two trigrams (Lightning above and Lightning below), but also of three bigrams—Spring in nature or the material realm, Autumn in the personal or social realm, and Winter in the spiritual or intentional realm.

Beyond the purely interpretive material this view provides, it also contains a predictive quality.

From Figure 8, we can see how Hexagram 1 *Provoking Change* contains within it the seeds of Hexagram 20 *Entering Service*: the Spring (7) in Nature is naturally changing into the Summer (9) of Nature, even as the Autumn (8) of Humanity is naturally changing into the Winter (6) of Humanity and the Winter (6) of Spirit is naturally changing into the Spring (7) of Spirit.

```
  ── ──         7
  ─────      SPRING      SPIRIT

  ── ──         6
  ── ──      WINTER      HUMANITY

  ─────         9
  ─────      SUMMER      NATURE
```

BIGRAMS OF HEXAGRAM 20 *ENTERING SERVICE*

These natural tendencies of the bigrams to follow one another in the cycle of seasons give rise to a wide-ranging field of exploration and study for practitioners.

> *5. THE CHANGES is a mirror that reflects both the macrocosm of all Creation and the microcosm of human nature. For this reason, male and female spirit warriors hone their attention on the whetstone of the Oracle. They bring their heart-minds into accord with its lifeway, following the line changes from the present into the future.*

Commentary

Because the symbols used in THE CHANGES are archetypal in nature, capturing the quintessential qualities and essences of things, they apply to every level of Thinking and Being. Women and men in every era bring the full brunt of attention to their relationship with the Oracle. This is so because there exists no more fundamental, direct or personal act of magic than a first-hand communion with the One. While many people search their whole lives to find the pathway into the divine presence, spirit warriors take that single step into the center of Being where knowledge and understanding fly into the heart-mind on the wings of light. Such practitioners have demonstrated over the millennia that entering into the divinatory moment with reverence and open-heartedness establishes a relationship wherein our thoughts and feelings are taken in by the Oracle and answered in the hexagrams. This is conceived of as a natural and spontaneous communion, much like a valley takes in our voice and throws back its echo without any contrived conscious effort.

Spirit warriors are men and women engaged in consciously defeating the *enemy-within*. They are those women and men consciously training themselves to unite their feminine and masculine halves in order to promote and share the good fortune of all. In their pursuit, they understand the *enemy-within* to be the self-defeating habits of thought, emotion and memory they have acquired through familial upbringing and social conditioning. Their training in this pursuit embodies a lifeway of *returning to the act of creation* and *rediscovering the true self*. This they attune themselves to, first, by perceiving the generative energy circulating in every level of Creation as symbolized by the trigrams and, second, by channeling their intent through the hexagrams to create the most positive future for all.

> *6. In times of calm, spirit warriors use its lessons to train their attention on defeating the enemy-within. In times of action, spirit warriors consult the Oracle in order to seek the best for themselves and all others at the same time. Treating all things as sacred, including themselves, spirit warriors depart the path of fate in favor of the good fortune lining the path of freedom.*

Commentary

THE CHANGES has two distinct but concurrent aspects. One is pure imagery and symbolism: the lines that make up the trigrams, hexagrams and line changes. The second is the interpretive material that accompanies the lines, trigrams and hexagrams: the commentary on each hexagram that analyzes the situation and points out the best way ahead based on the lessons handed down by the ancients. These lessons are instrumental in the training of spirit warriors: they provide the basis of the lifeway that opens the heart-mind to the authentic thoughts, emotions and memories of the true self. Studying these lessons and embodying their lifeway is the proper use of the text when circumstances are stable and no decisions need to be made. When times are chaotic and decisions demanded, then the proper use is to perform divinations and allow the *speaking of spirit* to guide action and intent.

The principal lesson of THE CHANGES is that everything is sacred, that matter *is* spirit, they we ourselves are sacred beings within a living Creation. As spirit warriors move these thoughts from their heads into their hearts, allowing themselves to *feel* the actuality of their immersion in divinity, they are no longer confused by the priorities and values of others—they cannot any longer be pushed or pulled along by convention or habit. Instead, they respond to each moment as a sacred peer within a universe of sacred peers, cut loose from precedents and inevitabilities both, the very embodiment of spontaneity, improvisation and light-heartedness.

—

Free even from the concept of *freedom*, spirit warriors set free their creative genius to accord with the living Creation within which they live and promote and share good fortune with all.

B. STUDYING THE CHANGES

Chapter III. *The Hexagram Interpretations*

1. The ILLUSTRATION depicts the lesson contained in each hexagram. The IMAGE describes the elements of its ILLUSTRATION and the INTERPRETATION points to the symbolism of each of its elements. The ACTION describes the interaction of forces at play within the situation depicted by the hexagram. The INTENT points to the underlying forces upon which spirit warriors focus their attention. The SUMMARY recapitulates the lesson expressed in its hexagram. The LINE CHANGES identify the present trends that are developing into the future situation.

<u>Commentary</u>

This section straightforwardly lays out the structure of the text of *The Toltec I Ching*, explaining the purpose of each part of the commentary accompanying each of the 64 hexagrams. Each of the hexagrams is accompanied by a pictorial text and written text. The pictorial text, or Illustration, utilizes the writing system of ancient Mesoamerica to express the dynamics of the hexagram. The written text then describes and interprets the pictorial text, after which it describes and interprets the hexagram and its line changes.

2. BENEFIT and NEED are the two fundamental poles of the spirit warrior's ethics. Meeting NEED with BENEFIT everywhere they go, spirit warriors accumulate inner power by keeping generative energy in constant circulation. The free flow of generative energy creates good fortune, damming up generative energy creates misfortune.

Commentary

The keystone of the spirit warrior's lifeway is *inspired action*, the ability to spontaneously respond to events in a way that furthers the development of the emerging world culture. In this sense, *inspired action* requires a code of ethics that embodies the values of the emerging world culture without creating artificial rules of conduct that impede the free flow of individual expression. Such an ethics is found in the code of *benefit-and-need*, which trains us to discern *need* wherever we find it and to address it appropriately with the kind and degree of *benefit* we have cultivated.

Spiritual intent (shen) directs generative energy (qi), which manifests as material form. By maintaining a spiritual intent that directs generative energy away from stagnating, spirit warriors consolidate inner power (jing). This inner power is identical in essence to the power of soil and water, whose purpose is *universal benefit*. By keeping generative energy flowing freely through them constantly, spirit warriors meet *need* with *benefit* everywhere they go, even as they further the accumulation and cultivation of inner power. Sharing good fortune brings good fortune, trying to keep it to oneself poisons it and turns it to misfortune.

3. Because things develop over time, they have stages, each of which has its own function and influence within the situation. The generative energy animating the situation is manifested in the distribution of YIN *and* YANG *lines. The* ACTION *and* INTERPRETATION *texts point to the ethical manner in which* NEED *can be addressed with* BENEFIT.

Commentary

Hexagrams are composed of six lines, which are viewed as organic stages of life that make up the developmental process of individuals, cultures and social institutions. They are counted from the bottom, up, because that is the way that plants grow. Understanding that the six lines of a hexagram demonstrate the way a situation develops over time is instrumental to going beyond an intellectual appreciation of the time.

Line / Stage	Issue / Meaning	Social Roles
6th *Elder* Culmination of the situation	Positive Disengagement Interdependence Wisdom	Mediators, Council, Advice Religions, Spirituality Sage, Mystic
5th *Mature Adult* Generally preferred place in hexagram	Authority Empowerment Directing Influence	The Powerful, The Ruling Class State, Judicial The Rich, Elite
4th *Young Adult* Bottom of upper trigram, a transition from below	Responsibility Independence	Bureaucracy Technocracy Corporations Local Officials
3rd *Adolescent* Top of lower trigram, often frustrated & uneasy	Alienation Separation	Dissidents, Artists
2nd *Child* Ruling line of the inner trigram, generally stable position	Trust Bonding	Social Service, Welfare Services Police, Military
1st *Infant* Entering the situation	Dependence Vulnerability	The Masses The Workers The Populace

FIGURE 9: THE SIX STAGES OF THE HEXAGRAM

Figure 9 illustrates this facet of development over time within the hexagram and how it is codified according to the context of the situation. When interpreting the hexagram in terms of time, for example, then the bottom line symbolizes *entering the situation* and the top line *culmination of the situation*. It is for this reason that the bottom and top lines are often thought of as outside the essential activity of the situation— this view has numerous exceptions, however, since there are many times when the very beginning or end of a situation are the most dynamic.

The six stages carry their respective issues that then combine with the nature of the broken (yin) and solid (yang) lines. When the changing broken and changing solid lines are taken into consideration, this means that any given hexagram is constructed of 24 possible elements: the six stages combined with the four types of lines.

Figure 10, below, depicts the so-called *Empty Hexagram*, the full potential of the Oracle's answer before the coins are thrown—

| LINE → | —x—
6 | ———
7 | — —
8 | —⊖—
9 |
STAGE ↓				
TOP STAGE				
FIFTH STAGE				
FOURTH STAGE				
THIRD STAGE				
SECOND STAGE				
BOTTOM STAGE				

FIGURE 10: THE 24 ELEMENTS OF THE HEXAGRAM

With each throw of the coins, the hexagram takes form, so that with the sixth throw, one of the 64 hexagrams has emerged from the realm of pure potential.

| LINE → | —x—
6 | ———
7 | — —
8 | —⊖—
9 |
STAGE ↓				
TOP STAGE			— —	
FIFTH STAGE	—x—			
FOURTH STAGE		———		
THIRD STAGE			— —	
SECOND STAGE			— —	
BOTTOM STAGE				—⊖—

FIGURE 11: CHART OF HEXAGRAM 1 *PROVOKING CHANGE*, WITH LINE CHANGES IN 1ˢᵗ AND 5ᵗʰ STAGES

Figure 11, above, depicts the results of a divination: Hexagram 1 *Provoking Change*, in which the bottom and fifth lines change. In its traditional form, the result is depicted as below—

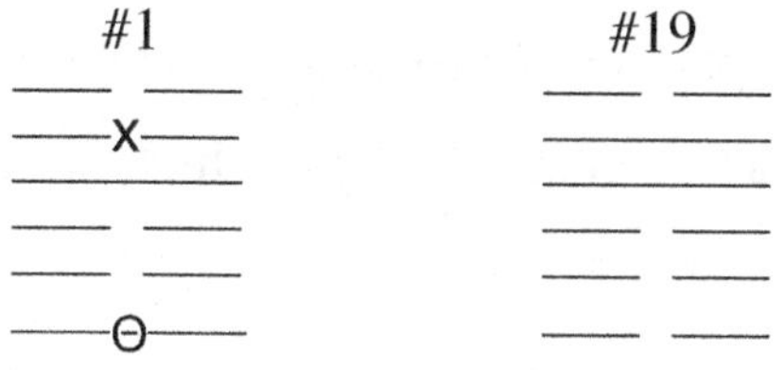

```
      #1                #19
  ———  ———          ———  ———
  ———x———           ———  ———
  ———  ———          ———  ———
  ———  ———          ———  ———
  ———  ———          ———  ———
  ———⊖———           ———  ———
```

47

When the first and fifth lines change in Hexagram 1, a secondary, or derived hexagram is produced by leaving all the *sevens* and *eights* unchanged while changing all the *sixes* and *nines* into their opposite, e.g., a changing broken line (6) changes into a solid line (7) and a changing solid line (9) changes into a broken line (8). In the example above, the two designated line changes in Hexagram 1 *Provoking Change* result in Hexagram 19 *Celebrating Passage*.

Generally speaking, the first hexagram of a divination depicts the present situation and the second hexagram depicts the future situation developing out of it. The line changes depict the specific transformations in the present situation that are bridging into the future situation.

The text accompanying each hexagram relays the ancients' lessons, which promote individual good fortune through the propagation of good fortune for all. Like water on its way to the sea, spirit warriors follow the line of least resistance while nurturing everything they touch along the way. Those attuned to the current of universal benefit sense true *need* the way water senses a waiting seed—intellectual discernment gives way to spiritual intuition in the moment-to-moment recognition of, and response to, *need*. The text accompanying the hexagrams describes the ethical response of *benefit* as it applies to the circumstances and conditions unique to each particular hexagram.

> *4. The enemy-within dams up generative energy, refusing to meet the illness of* NEED *with the medicine of* BENEFIT. *This causes one's inner power to drain away, creating ever greater* NEED *in one's own life. The cure for this illness is found in the spirit warrior's acceptance of the sacredness of all things: In this acceptance lies the panacea of* BENEFIT.

Commentary

The *enemy-within* is defined as *the self-defeating habits of thought, emotion and memory*. Individuals have an enemy-within, as do groups of people, social institutions and entire cultures. In point of fact, the whole of humankind has its very real and active enemy-within, which is the source of a painful alienation from nature and its own mystical nature.

The lack of universal goodwill and unconditional acceptance dams up the very *benefit* that has to flow among all if humaneness and justice are to prevail. What is true on the individual level holds true on the collective levels: damming up *good fortune* makes us poorer, unhappier, and, ultimately, brings us misfortune. Expanding on the model established in Figure 4: Illnesses and Medicines, above, the remedy for this illness is *not* continuing to act as we have. Breaking through the sense of encapsulation that keeps us alienated from nature, others and ourselves depends on sensing first-hand the living sacredness of everything. How can we enter into the lifeway of the ancients without stepping onto the road of living light, life and love that they explored from origin to destination?

> *5. The feminine and masculine halves of the spirit warrior take turns coming to the fore in order to live a fulfilling life, fulfill a living purpose, and share it with allies. The enemy-within fixates on one half of the spirit warrior, meeting every situation with the same one-sided response to circumstances. Spirit warriors enjoy good fortune because they find the natural equilibrium in their inner duality.*

Commentary

The broken and solid lines replace one another, marking the path of change between hexagrams, just as our feminine and masculine halves take turns directing our attention, intention and actions. Living equilibrium is forever dynamic, never a static artificial balance—it upsets the static in order to create new and more adaptive wholes. The six stages of a hexagram relate to the six stages of an individual's psyche, all of which exist at the same time. The difference between the stages lies in which are in the foreground of attention, which are in the background of attention, and which are changing to their opposite.

6 = waking up	emerging	*will be* an issue	coming into foreground
7 = active	conscious	*is* an issue	in foreground
8 = subliminal	unconscious	*not* an issue	in background
9 = going to sleep	submerging	*won't be* an issue	fading into background

FIGURE 12: MARKING SHIFTS OF ATTENTION

Dynamic creative equilibrium lies in the uncontrived and spontaneous alternation of our feminine and masculine halves at each of the six stages of our situation, both internal and external, both individual and collective. Figure 4: Illnesses and Medicines, above, provides a firm foundation for the conscious practice of this alternation until it is fully internalized and completely unselfconscious.

Chapter IV. *The Esoteric Lessons of The Changes*

> *1. THE CHANGES is a microcosm of the mystical PATTERN OF ORDER AND CHANCE underlying SPIRIT and NATURE: It leaps beyond itself into the Unknowable, carrying the spirit warrior into the realm of transcendent experience.*

Commentary

On the cosmological scale, dynamic creative equilibrium arises from the interplay of the forces seeking *stability through predictable order* and *metamorphosis through random chance*. Neither of these two forces ever dominates to the complete exclusion of the other—it is their interaction, like the interference waves of pond ripples, that self-organizes local pockets of *times of greater stability* and *times of greater metamorphosis*. The *union* of this great duality of cosmos and chaos constitutes a *pattern* that is both alive and aware, much as the DNA of the genetic code is both alive and aware: pure awareness is pure information without any boundaries—self-aware information is the inevitable result, as is unbounded communion of awareness. The *Pattern of Order and Chance* is a mystical Being who gives birth to the great duality of cosmos and chaos and, simultaneously, is given birth by the union of cosmos and chaos.

That there is a pattern to order is clear. That there is a pattern to chance is obscure. We can see that there are mutations within the genetic code, despite the fixity of the code. We cannot necessarily predict those mutations or their consequences ahead of time but we can appreciate that they are part of the code itself. The *Pattern*, in other words, allows from the very beginning for its own unpredictable evolution—it seeks its own transcendence by incorporating the unpredictable into its intrinsic structure. And it is not, of course, given birth by the genetic code, since the genetic code is but one of its many manifestations.

THE CHANGES is likewise a self-contained manifestation of the *Pattern of Order and Chance*. It essentializes the *Pattern* in the same way that the RNA messenger code does DNA. By means of its archetypal structure and dynamics, THE CHANGES is able to symbolize the infinitely complex and evolving universe. This it accomplishes by mirroring the subsensorial *generative energy* that circulates below the threshold of the five senses until it emerges in material form.

This process of emergence is similar to a thought, feeling, sensation, memory, etc., that has resided in the unconscious suddenly becoming conscious: the unconscious element that has existed in a nonperceptible state has nonetheless been exerting its influence on behavior or mood, its unexpressed energy building tension that is finally released as the element crosses the threshold of liminality and becomes conscious. Just as there are individuals who train themselves to be unusually sensitive to unconscious thoughts, feelings, memories, etc., there are individuals who train themselves to be more sensitive to the circulation of generative energy: those who read symbolic behavior of others and thus divine the unconscious dynamics beneath the conscious surface are performing the same type of activity as those who read the symbolic behavior of spirit as it manifests in all forms of nature. Such spirit warriors have since ancient times been called *diviners* because they are trained to divine the intent of spirit, thereby foreseeing the direction and momentum of change in the natural and human realms.

In the same way that a great ship pushes water ahead of itself as a prow wake in which dolphins sport, the PATTERN OF ORDER AND CHANCE pushes change ahead of itself as a purposeful future in which diviners explore. Similarly, just as there lies the vastness of the open sea encompassing ship and prow wake and dolphins, there lies the vast oceanic *Great Mystery* encompassing the PATTERN OF ORDER AND CHANCE and purposeful future and diviners. THE CHANGES symbolizes the living awareness that is the PATTERN OF ORDER AND CHANCE: in its actions, it mirrors the way that Order and Chance alternate to create ever-new potential, calling it forth it from THE UNMANIFEST.

ORDER	— —	REALIZED	FORM	NATURE	STABILITY	FATE
CHANCE	————	POTENTIAL	FORMLESS	SPIRIT	METAMORPHOSIS	FREEDOM

FIGURE 13: THE PATTERN OF ORDER AND CHANCE

Standing at the gate, observing the comings and goings of all things as they arrive from and return to THE UNMANIFEST in their own time, spirit warriors become attuned to the transcendent realm of timeless creation. Since ancient times, this gate has been called The Estuary, for it is the place where the river meets the ocean — where the freshwater of the Known terrain mingles with the saltwater tides of the Unknowable sea.

Here is the secret standpoint of the diviner, for just as freshwater and saltwater are both *water* yet impossible to mistake one for the other, mortal and immortal awareness are both *awareness* yet immediately discernable from one another. The Estuary is that sacred place wherein diviners dwell, neither in time nor in eternity but in that shared space where their ever-circulating currents create an ephemeral mirror-like awareness of what passes between them.

Figure 13, above, illustrates the principal symbols of the PATTERN OF ORDER AND CHANCE and their associations to the solid and broken lines of THE CHANGES.

> *2. THE CHANGES reveals the unchanging nature of SPIRIT and the unchanging spirit of NATURE: SPIRIT is none other than the invisible half of NATURE, just as NATURE is none other than the visible half of SPIRIT. In the changing lines lies the secret relationship between mortality and immortality. The union of the masculine and feminine halves produces the spiritual embryo: Once the spiritual twin can journey on its own, one becomes an intimate of birth and death. Roaming in the land of The Changeless even as we perform our everyday tasks, we commune equally with the souls of the living and the souls of the dead.*

Commentary

Figure 13, above, makes clear that Nature is symbolized by broken lines and Spirit by solid lines. This reflects their essential unchanging identities: Everyone and everything has a visible half and an invisible half, a body of Nature and a soul of Spirit. But the lines grow and incorporate more of the qualities of their opposites over time, an interchange reflected in the changing lines: broken lines change into solid lines and solid lines change into broken lines. This interchange symbolizes the secret way that nature changes into spirit and spirit into nature—the profoundly mysterious and hidden path by which the mortal body becomes immortal spirit and immortal spirit becomes mortal body.

The spiritualization of matter and the materialization of spirit: such is the secret path by which the innate perfectibility of all things advances through ever-deeper and ever-higher realms, sweeping like a wind through every chasm and valley, every storm and open sky. In the changing lines are hidden the body of the soul and the soul of the body, the feminine half and the masculine half of every *nonduality*.

The interchangeability of the qualities of these two halves on the individual scale of the lived life results in a blending of characteristics, like the roots of two mighty trees interwoven deep underground, that forms an unbreakable bond between the soul of the body and the body of the soul: uniting the seeming opposites into the personal *nonduality* is a creative act, a birth, that mirrors the cosmological union of the Great Duality into the ongoing *Act of Creation*. What is born here on the personal level is the *intentional body*: It is for this reason that it has been said of old, *Just as there is a mind within the mind, there is a body outside the body.*

The intentional body is, at first, unstable, like a newborn deer trying to find its legs and keep its balance—unsure of the realm in which it lives, the intentional body struggles to find its footing and maintain continuity of awareness. With familiarity and concentration, though, it gains strength and agility, no less than the fawn bounding and leaping within the safety of the herd—as it emerges within the *intentional landscape*, the intentional body begins to move among the landmarks and other intentional bodies with cautious deliberation. Finally, with patience and practice, it moves with all the grace and inner power of a great stag perfectly at home in the wilderness—coming into contact with the intentional bodies of all those who have ever lived, the spiritual twin evolves into a fully-formed *purpose* that must align itself with the *Universal Purpose* of the *One Intent* if it is to create good fortune wherever it goes. It is in this realm that we build great alliances and set in motion *formulations of generative energy* to take form and enter the flow of history.

3. THE CHANGES reveals that the original nature of human being is identical to the sacred WAY of SPIRIT and NATURE. Wisdom is found beneath the artificial layers of culture, history, and personality: Human perceptions are made of the same material as SPIRIT and NATURE. The enemy-within is made of all one's self-defeating perceptions, amplified by all the self-defeating lessons drawn from the social environment: failing to commune with one's true self, with HUMANITY, with NATURE, with SPIRIT, all out of fear and distrust of life—this is the road of misfortune that leads to a wasted lifetime. Spirit warriors seek the true self beneath the facade of the enemy-within, harmonizing with its purpose for taking up this lifetime. They bring their intent into accord with that purpose, they bring their actions into accord with that intent. They know the outflowing cycle of generative energy on the path of fate and choose instead the path of freedom.

No longer confined to the realm of birth and death, they are at peace, filled with the love of the world. They do not strive, but follow the path of least resistance marked out by meaningful coincidences. They radiate gratitude for being part of such a wondrous creation, returning the loving-kindness of SPIRIT and NATURE with benevolence toward all. Allowing themselves to be loved by that which is greater than themselves, they can love.

Commentary

The wisdom teachings of the perennial truth favor no one: like rain and sunlight and soil, they nurture every seed without bias. There is no special knowledge or esoteric skill that privileges one soul over another. It is simply the authenticity of conscious perfectibility that forever pulls the sincere individual from one station to the next. This natural tendency toward awakening sets the compass points of the intentional body's sense of direction: the path is wide and straight and level for those who mirror within themselves the sacred marriage of Spirit and Nature. Shedding the conventional domestication of human nature, such spirit warriors focus their intention on extinguishing the self-defeating habits of thought, emotion and memory that would chain them to a lifetime of trivialization.

This mirroring within the microcosm of the macrocosm is inevitable because the very substance of human perceptions is made of the same substance making up all other phenomena in the universe. It is in this sense that it has been said of old, *There is no inside and outside.*

What we are perceiving with is the same substance as *what we are perceiving.* They have the same intrinsic pattern, the same essential makeup. This is what makes it possible for us to see mountains and rivers where there are, in reality, only subatomic particles: our senses have the same-sized holes between things as the substance making up this mesocosm within which our bodies exist. The ocean of generative energy (*qi*), in other words, gives form to everything in the universe, including our senses. It is for this reason that the eight trigrams are said to be senses: they establish the bridge between our perceptions and the world of phenomena because they *embody the archetypal pattern of order and chance making up both.*

As manifestations of generative energy, each of the trigrams contains its own specific allotment of *qi*. When pictured in their archetypal relationships of opposite-complements, the trigrams are considered to be suspended in their timeless realm, prior to actually manifesting phenomena in the timebound realm (See Figure 1: Book 1, Chapter 2, Section 3).

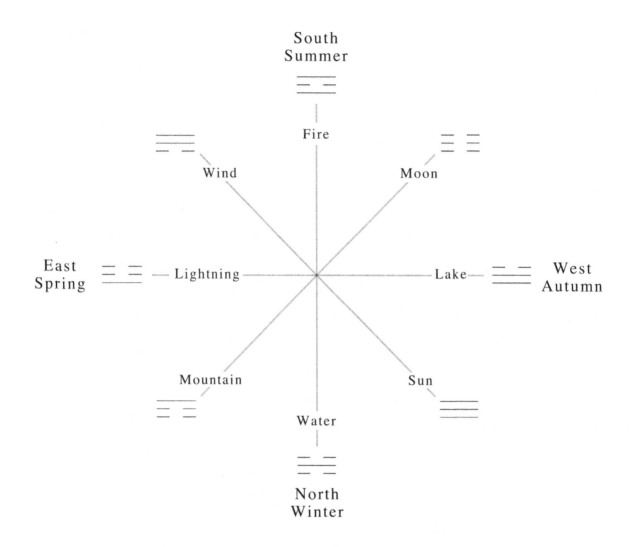

Figure 14: The King Wen Compass Arrangement of the Trigrams

Once *qi* has entered the realm of phenomena, however, it moves in a linear fashion, as represented by the cyclical progression of trigrams in Figure 14, above.

Here, the ordinary *outflowing of qi* is depicted as beginning with the birth of things in the trigram Lightning and developing in a clockwise direction until death in the trigram Mountain (See: Book 1, Chapter 2, Sections 5 and 6). This cyclic course of development is called the *path of fate*, the predictable course of the birth, waxing, waning and death of ordinary existence. The alternative to the *path of fate* is the *path of freedom*, marked by the counter-clockwise movement from the trigram Mountain back to the origin in the trigram Lightning. As such, the *path of freedom* is the practice of moving backward in time, starting at the point of death and returning to the point of birth. This is a movement embodying the *cultivation of qi*, the effects of which increase health, vitality, longevity and well-being.

Similar in principle to the backward-moving circulation of the Primal Arrangement (See Figure 1: Book 1, Chapter 2, Section 3), the present case nonetheless differs in aim. Whereas the practice associated with the Primal Arrangement is essentially spiritual, manifesting the individual realization of the *Return of the Many to the One*, the practice associated with the King Wen Arrangement is essentially energetic, manifesting the physical and emotional benefits of the cultivation of generative energy.

In both cases, however, the practice involves *moving into each trigram in turn* as if each were a *Season* in which one is fully immersed. Occupying the trigrams in this fashion requires sensitizing oneself to the archetypal qualities of each and then moving one's intentional body wholly into the *Season* of each in turn (See Figure 3: Book 1, Chapter 2, Section 11). For this reason, the backward-circulation of *qi* has long been called the *True Year*.

> *4. THE CHANGES mirrors the living PATTERN OF ORDER AND CHANCE underlying SPIRIT and NATURE: Because the PATTERN embodies the generative energy that shapes both FORM and FORMLESS, all phenomena, from the most dense to the most sublime, are reflected clearly in THE CHANGES. Because all things come from a common origin, they share a common purpose. Because all things flow from a common source, they share a common destiny. Going forward to know the end is accomplished by going back to know the beginning: The Changes reveals the archetypal structure of change set in motion with the Act of Creation. Phenomena appear and disappear because they are changes against the backdrop of THE CHANGELESS—they are not solid things. Like whitecaps on the open sea, everything arises and falls back into the Current of Fate. Radiant awareness alone, the font from which the living PATTERN OF ORDER AND CHANCE itself arises, has the freedom to move between the structures of change. THE CHANGES is the map of order and the Oracle the voice of chance: Internalizing THE CHANGES, the spirit warrior journeys at will. Just as the perennial truth is an open secret that must adapt to the mind of each age if it is to continue living, THE CHANGES is a living relict of The Beginning that must adapt to each new time and place if it is to continue all the way through.*

Commentary

This section is concerned with the non-dual nature of all things as it expresses itself across the entire spectrum of manifold manifestations.

From the highest to the lowest, from the nearest to the furthest, from the smallest to the largest, from the most concrete to the most abstract, from the most cohesive to the most chaotic, from the most familiar to the most mysterious, from the most mundane to the most holy—nothing is outside the Indivisible. Nothing, therefore, is beyond the influence of other elements within the Indivisible—which is to say, nothing is beyond healing or redemption. See FIGURE 15: DIAGRAM OF THE INDIVISIBLE, below.

The *PATTERN OF ORDER AND CHANCE* is understood as the system of symbols depicting the Emanations of Creation (See FIGURE 5: Book 2, Chapter 2, Section 4), which expresses the way in which the One manifests itself through a process of doubling until it becomes the 8 trigrams and the 64 hexagrams. The sequence of the hexagrams marks the flow of change on the archetypal level of spiritual cause-and-effect: This sequence is called the MAP OF ORDER, since it depicts the way in which generative energy unfolds from beginning to end and back again to beginning. It carries things along, the *GREAT CURRENT* washing down from the headwaters in PROVOKING CHANGE toward the sea in SAFEGUARDING LIFE. Without exerting the effort to give birth to the intentional body, people are swept up in the history of the times and carried away from the freedom to create their own lives. The Oracle, however, offers a way out of the conventional lifetime: By introducing the element of chance into the Way of Order, the Oracle revitalizes it by infusing it throughout with *meaningful coincidence*.

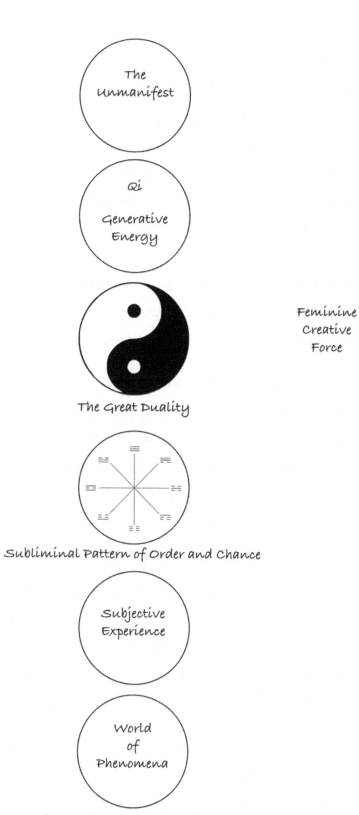

FIGURE 15: DIAGRAM OF THE INDIVISIBLE

The act of consulting the Oracle with the coins in the ritual called, *The Forest of Fire Pearls*, allows us to see our place in the MAP OF ORDER and move forward or backward within the sequence rather than be carried along by the forces of fate (See FIGURE 16: THE SEQUENCE OF HEXAGRAMS, below). With practice, we gain intimacy with *THE CHANGES* and find the *PATTERN OF ORDER AND CHANCE* within ourselves: It is at this point that we consciously step onto the Path of Freedom, since our ability to assess our surroundings has grown manifoldly more accurate and our continuum of possible responses has multiplied exponentially. The first-hand experience of the diviner's state is extraordinarily *sensory*: It is a *feeling of fitting-with* rather than an abstract concept of place or time. And it is an *intuitive abandon*, a spontaneous response to events that seems to come through us rather than from us. This shift of the diviner's awareness occurs because of a voluntary stepping aside of the conscious personality in order to allow the vastness of the Oracle's awareness to come through us. It is this awareness that we as diviners come to share with the Oracle—an awareness called since ancient times, the *Mind of Heaven*.

Clear, without disturbance. Immediate, without contrivance. Purposeful, without aim. Reverential, without fixation. Untroubled, without forethought. Careful, without calculation. Benevolent, without cause. Such is the *Mind of Heaven* that diviners cultivate by steeping themselves in the thoughts and intentions of the Oracle. By sensing the *PATTERN* within ourselves, we are able to extinguish the self-defeating habits of thought, emotion and memory holding us to the *Path of Fate* and, thereby, be welcomed into the *Mind of Heaven*.

Clarifying the generative energy of their heart-minds, diviners learn the secret pathways of chance, opening the *Gate of Coming and Going*: This is the mountain pass, so to speak, whereby we leave all we have known in this lifetime and return to the pure uncharted territory of Original Nature. Understanding how awareness returns to *The Beginning* allows us to stand before the eternal Act of Creation and witness the emergence of *THE CHANGES* from the flames of *THE UNCHANGING*. Timeless as its essence is, its form nonetheless needs to be revivified with the passing generations in order to be attuned to the *Spirit of the Age*.

Diviners are those leading the way to this attunement of *THE CHANGES* with the *Spirit of the Age*, carrying within their radiant awareness the seed of *THE PATTERN* that will bear fruit and new seed in its turn, spiritualizing matter as it materializes spirit.

#1 Provoking Change	#33 Accepting Instruction
#2 Sensing Creation	#34 Evoking Opposite
#3 Recognizing Ancestry	#35 Holding Back
#4 Mirroring Wisdom	#36 Stabilizing Communion
#5 Restoring Wholeness	#37 Penetrating Confusion
#6 Fostering Self-Sacrifice	#38 Dissolving Artifice
#7 Compelling Motive	#39 Reviving Tradition
#8 Harmonizing Duality	#40 Adapting Experience
#9 Uprooting Fear	#41 Feigning Compliance
#10 Unifying Inspiration	#42 Interpreting Insight
#11 Attracting Allies	#43 Going Beyond
#12 Seeing Ahead	#44 Refining Instinct
#13 Concentrating Attention	#45 Casting Off
#14 Unlocking Evolution	#46 Honoring Contentment
#15 Belonging Together	#47 Making Individual
#16 Renewing Devotion	#48 Moving Source
#17 Guiding Force	#49 Staying Open
#18 Resolving Paradox	#50 Narrowing Aim
#19 Celebrating Passage	#51 Living Essence
#20 Entering Service	#52 Growing Certainty
#21 Cultivating Character	#53 Mastering Reason
#22 Sharing Memory	#54 Repeating Test
#23 Wielding Passion	#55 Internalizing Purity
#24 Revealing Knowledge	#56 Recapturing Vision
#25 Radiating Intent	#57 Defying Uncertainty
#26 Dignifying Ambition	#58 Dawning Existence
#27 Trusting Intuition	#59 Developing Potential
#28 Synchronizing Movement	#60 Changing Alliances
#29 Sustaining Resilience	#61 Strengthening Integrity
#30 Transforming Extinction	#62 Conceiving Spirit
#31 Embracing Noninterference	#63 Awakening Self-Sufficiency
#32 Controlling Confrontation	#64 Safeguarding Life

FIGURE 16: THE SEQUENCE NUMBERS OF THE HEXAGRAMS

Chapter V. *The Sacred Way of Duality*

1. There is a secret Way that unites every Duality.

Commentary

Even a sage can tell if water is hot or cold. To see the unitary nature of all things does not make people less discerning—in fact, it makes them capable of ever finer distinctions within the indivisible One. Water may be hot or cold but it is still water. This is how all things are. The distinctions between things are real but temporary, while their common essence is real and eternal.

The Morning Star and the Evening Star are both the planet Venus. To appreciate the dual nature of the One is to celebrate the *Love of Union* binding all things together. The planet Venus spends approximately 260 days as the Morning Star and then disappears behind the sun, whereupon it emerges to spend approximately 260 days as the Evening Star before disappearing behind the sun again and starting the cycle over. This is how all things are. The Morning Star and the Evening Star appear to be two wholly different things occupying two entirely different places—yet they are one and the same planet.

One eye sees the changing, the other eye see the unchanging. The dwelling place of difference is thought, the dwelling place of sameness is thought. To see that both change and nonchange, both difference and sameness, exist only in thought is to understand that radiant awareness itself is part of the oceanic reality of Being, inseparable from all the objects of thought it entertains. The Great Non-Duality is holy. The Great Duality is holy. The sacredness of the sperm unites with the sacredness of the egg and the sacredness of a child is born: How can the living duality, itself born of the *Love of Union*, be less sacred than the next generation of living non-duality it gives rise to?

How does one get the milk of a snow leopard? So long as the snow leopard is secretive and elusive, it remains impossible to obtain its milk. The secret Way is simply to be a snow leopard cub.

2. It nurtures everything without preference, it brings all things home without exception.

Commentary

The One gives room for every intention to develop. It is like the soil and the rain and the sunlight, which provide a place for every seed to take root and grow among all other plants. To fully sense the *open substance* of the universal field of generative energy is to feel first-hand the *lushness* of the ground of realization ever before us. It is for this reason that it has long been called, the *Seedbed of Desire*: Whatever intention is sowed therein is given the room to thrive amid all other intentions. In this way, individuals are given every opportunity to realize their fullest potential.

Nothing is ever lost. Like a vast net stretched out beneath all Creation, the One catches all things upon their dissolution and returns them to their origin in the *Love of Union* from whence they sprung. For this reason, the Way has long been called the *Unborn*: The One is Itself not ever born, so it cannot ever die—because it is Itself the Indivisible, none of its elements can ever die. Things come into and go out of manifestation but that is merely transformation of form: The return to the other side of manifestation has long been called the *Warrior's Homecoming*. To enter voluntarily into the realm of birth and death, to pass through its maze of shadows and illusions, to endure the joys and sorrows of mortality—all this has long been considered the quest of the spirit warrior.

> *3. It is wide and straight and clear but many are mislead away from compassion and wisdom by their enemy-within.*

Commentary

The Way of the spirit warrior is the path of every individual. Though not all recognize it or take up the discipline to pass through this lifetime unscathed, there is but this one path upon which each wayfarer meets their own enemy-within. Although the enemy-within is the entire range of self-defeating habits of thought, emotion and memory harbored by the individual, it is those that betray our true nature with justifications for self-interest and willfulness that are the concerns of this section.

Our self-defeating habits delude us into thinking that humaneness and justice are unattainable ideals in a world of greed and force—into resigning ourselves to the corrupting influence of materialism and cultural upbringing.

But this is no different than the self-defeating habits that delude us into thinking that humaneness and justice are attainable ideals in a world of greed and force—no different than those driving us to rail against every imperfection we find in the world around us. Apathy is no different than self-righteousness: Both lead away from the path of compassion and wisdom.

For spirit warriors, compassion and wisdom are both based on communion with the One. When we identify with the Living Whole, we care for each thing within it as if it were our only grandchild. This *being-with* the One permits us to open our hearts to the true *need* of each thing and to open our minds to the most authentic response that addresses that *need* with true *benefit*. Feeling true *need* and responding with true *benefit* is the union of compassion and wisdom—is the ideal embodiment of humaneness and justice.

The Way of compassion and wisdom is level and wide-open but many step off the path out of fear and distrust, a fundamental sense of separation from the world that seems to justify placing their own needs above those of others and their own personal knowledge above the accumulated wisdom of the ages. Spirit warriors respect the cunning of the enemy-within, which is able to shape-shift like smoke, always taking some new form of self-defeating habits in order to forestall the inevitable breakthrough experience that shatters one's chrysalis and opens one's wings to the pure breeze blowing throughout the whole world of loving-kindness.

> *4. The Way of the One is universally benevolent but its twists of fate are difficult to anticipate. It is the very ocean of life within which all dwell but its concerns are infinitely greater than the concerns of human beings. Its ennobling emanation, coursing throughout every atom of creation like the single sea of immaterial water, is itself the perfecting agent at work on all things. It recognizes no distinctions and so is its own Way.*

Commentary

The intentional field is a filled with the intentions of all those who have ever lived. So, although the Way Itself is universally benevolent, the conflicting and dissonant intentions influencing the manifestations of *qi* utilize that benevolence in ways that counteract one another. This inability to harmonize our intentions with the universally benevolent intent of the One is the cause of all our avoidable suffering.

It is for this reason that spirit warriors take up the practice of purifying their generative energy by extinguishing their self-defeating habits of thought, emotion and memory: The naturally-occurring universally benevolent intent of the One lodges in the heart-mind that has reverted to calm quiet.

The calm and quiet heart-mind dwells in its own innate perfectibility. Diviners who attune themselves to the benevolence of the Way exude magnanimous *qi*.

> *5. All the NATURE and SPIRIT ever created exists in the present moment—only their forms change. Like a bubbling wellspring of creation, the Way of the One pours forth the immaterial fire that keeps the spark of light burning within all in this eternal moment—only the outside ever changes.*

Commentary

Neither the material nor the energetic can be created or destroyed. Therefore, everything that exists has always existed, what is present now was present at the Act of Creation. What was created at the Beginning is precisely what is before us now. That we ourselves exist now means that we have existed since the very Beginning. As part and parcel of the Whole, we need only turn our gaze inward upon ourselves to see the unfolding of Creation—the outward gaze merely moves from separation to separation, from one temporary form to all other temporary forms.

No time is lost between lives: Radiant awareness returns to form as if from a deep sleep, the awakened mind begins where it last left off. The continuity of awareness across multiple forms flows from the *Well of Memory* hidden in the backmost recesses of the *Inner Cavern*. This is the Way of the One, the Two-Fold Road, running ever forward into an ever-more perfect realization of potential even as it runs ever backward to the eternal Act of Creation. Some say it is a circular road, like a great serpent swallowing its own tail. Others say it runs in both directions only when one stands perfectly and utterly still. Yet others say we are constructing the road ourselves with our every thought. But all agree that the Way of the Indivisible is an *Inner Compass* pointing to the immortal awareness awakening again in this present moment.

> *6. The catalyst of the Way's momentum is the turning of the Wheel of Inner Duality.*

Commentary

All things contain their own contradiction. It is impossible to speak of the One without speaking of the veil of paradox behind which its unitary nature is hidden. The way in which the subject-object illusion must be overcome in order to experience first-hand the interconnectedness of all things, for example, speaks to the peculiar intent of the One: Attested to by innumerable sages and mystics and poets of every age, the One is itself an act of sacred play—is itself a Sacred Game. That the lived experience of a body resides in an immaterial spirit imperceptible to the body, as another example, hints at the playful nature of Creation: In a cosmic game of leapfrog, understanding and love grow ever greater as the known and unknown perpetually give birth to one another. That all minds are One Mind, as a third example, demonstrates that the players within this Sacred Game must voluntarily sacrifice their most powerful piece in order to advance to each new higher stage of play: In a universal game of hide-and-seek, *Everything is the One* that remains hidden from us until we quit seeking It and begin looking at our blindfold. This is the Sacred Game of the One, the Way of Self-Remembering, the exploration of every possible combination of parts in order to create the most perfect mirror of the Whole.

The One creates all things in its image and likeness, which is to say, with an inherent paradox at their core that drives them to create their own works of self-discovery. From within, these works of self-discovery are called a *lifetime*. From without, these works of self-discovery are called *art*. Regardless of the form taken, the Way of the One is set in motion by its own act of self-discovery.

The One is not a machine producing dead matter out of which arises life, out of which arises consciousness, out of which arises self-awareness, out of which arises self-transcendence. Rather, the One is Alive and Aware, the World Soul, Gaia, Spirit, the Great Mystery, the Creator, the Creative Forces, the One Mind, Divine Intelligence: It contains its own contradiction because it would otherwise fall into stasis and decay and that is not Its intent. The *Wheel of Inner Duality* turns and its paradoxical nature opens and closes the *Gate of Coming and Going*. (See FIGURE 17: THE WHEEL OF INNER DUALITY, below).

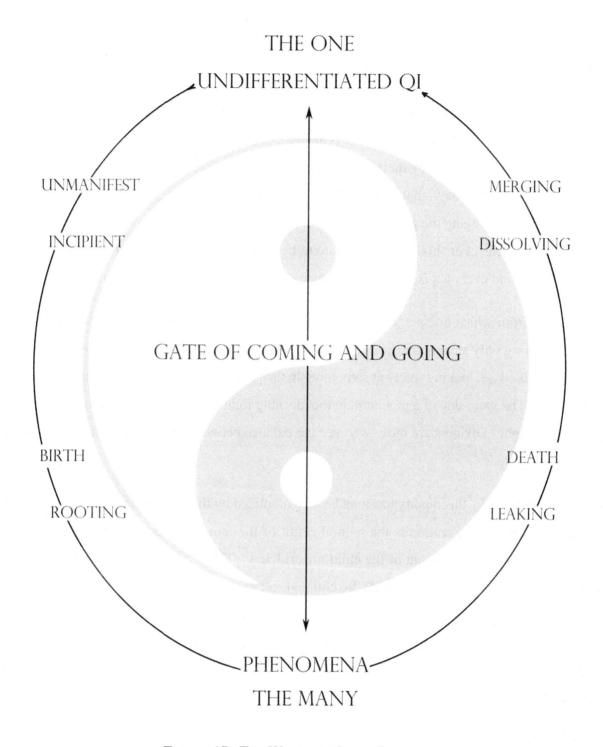

THE ONE

UNDIFFERENTIATED QI

UNMANIFEST   MERGING

INCIPIENT   DISSOLVING

GATE OF COMING AND GOING

BIRTH   DEATH

ROOTING   LEAKING

PHENOMENA

THE MANY

FIGURE 17: THE WHEEL OF INNER DUALITY

7. Yang generative energy conceives potential, Yin generative energy realizes potential.

Commentary

Once the One is moved to acts of self-discovery, it begins and finishes things. Yang *qi* is that half of the One which brings new potential to light. Yin *qi* is that half of the One which brings potential to its individual realization. Yang and yin *qi* are by their nature woven together in complex ways. Dawn, for example, is the yang *qi* initiating a new day—but it is also the yin *qi* bringing the night to an end. The birth of a child, likewise, is the yin *qi* bringing the gestation period to an end—but it is also the yang *qi* bringing individual potential into the world. For this reason, it has long been said that nothing is purely yang *qi* or yin *qi*—rather, every thing and every act *is* a nuanced balance of the two Creative Forces at play.

The perspective from which one perceives the Creative Forces bears strongly on how one identifies yang and yin *qi*. Looking only at something as being in the process of beginning, one will not see the attendant yin *qi* present. Likewise, looking solely at something in the process of ending, one will not see the attendant yang *qi* at hand. The yang side of a mountain in the morning light proves to be the yin side of the mountain in the afternoon light. Diviners are those who see the balance between the Creative Forces at play in each thing and each act.

Within the individual life, this duality has long been symbolized by the masculine half and feminine half of human nature. This symbolization is the natural result of the *father* and *mother* archetypes that play so formative a role in the development of the child's worldview. The functional value of this symbolization lies in the individual's ability to transcend conventional roles associated with gender, thereby mirroring the One's act of self-discovery as a constant shifting and re-balancing of the masculine creative force and the feminine creative force. In Figure 17, above, this inherent relationship is depicted in the two "eyes" of the two "fish" swimming in opposite directions: The light half of the symbol is a yang fish with a yin eye, while the dark half of the symbol is a yin fish with a yang eye.

See also: Book II, Part 1, Chapter 1, Sections 4-6.

8. THE CHANGES reveals itself as Number governing the mystic PATTERN OF ORDER and the future unfolding out of it. The Oracle reveals itself as Presence governing the living PATTERN OF CHANCE and the freedom created out of it.

Commentary

This section expands on the concepts of freedom and fate first introduced in Book I, Chapter I, Section 2. Here we have specific correlations between *THE CHANGES*, number, order and fate on the one hand, and *THE ORACLE*, communion, chance and freedom on the other.

THE CHANGES in this sense refers to the sequence of hexagrams beginning with #1 *PROVOKING CHANGE* and ending with #64 *SAFEGUARDING LIFE*. This sequence depicts the natural unfolding of generative energy in the present Age. It is orderly, following the course of spiritual cause-and-effect as each period of time is brought about as a reaction to the previous one. In the case of #1 *PROVOKING CHANGE*, it is the natural response to #64 *SAFEGUARDING LIFE* that ending the previous Age. Each of the hexagrams is in actuality a number ranging from 0 to 63, which are called QI NUMBERS and represent the allotment of generative energy each carries. These numbers are distinct from the ordinal numbers running from #1 to #64 in the sequence of hexagrams: They are cardinal numbers representing the very identity of each of the hexagrams. The SEQUENCE NUMBERS #1 to #64 are based on a transmutation of the King Wen arrangement of the hexagrams handed down from the Chou dynasty (See Figure 16, above). The cardinal numbers 0 to 63 are the natural numbers of the hexagrams that were, by tradition, handed down across the generations from the divine ancestor Fu Xi to the great Song dynasty philosopher Shao Yung (See Figure 18, below).

Because the QI NUMBERS mark the *allotment of qi* each hexagram bears, they are direct expressions of the specific *quality of fate* that gives each hexagram its individual nature. So, while the 64 QI NUMBERS are the *identities* of the 64 hexagrams, the 64 *qualities of fate* are symbolized by the *names* of the hexagrams and their associated *illustrations*. The *qualities of fate* are, in turn, determined by the fundamental synergistic interaction of each hexagram's upper trigram and lower trigram (See Book I, Chapter III, Sections 7-11).

The Qi Numbers of the Hexagrams

#51	#24	#27	#25	#3	#42	#21	#17
0	1	2	3	4	5	6	7

#16	#2	#23	#12	#8	#20	#35	#45
8	9	10	11	12	13	14	15

#62	#15	#52	#33	#39	#53	#56	#31
16	17	18	19	20	21	22	23

#34	#11	#26	#1	#5	#9	#14	#43
24	25	26	27	28	29	30	31

#40	#7	#4	#6	#29	#59	#64	#47
32	33	34	35	36	37	38	39

#32	#46	#18	#44	#48	#57	#50	#28
40	41	42	43	44	45	46	47

#55	#36	#22	#13	#63	#37	#30	#49
48	49	50	51	52	53	54	55

#54	#19	#41	#10	#60	#61	#38	#58
56	57	58	59	60	61	62	63

FIGURE 18: THE FU XI ARRANGEMENT OF THE HEXAGRAMS

In Figure 18, above, the number *below* each hexagram is its QI NUMBER and the number *above* each hexagram is its SEQUENCE NUMBER (See Figure 16, above).

By way of example, the hexagram comprised of the upper trigram Lightning and lower trigram Lightning is SEQUENCE NUMBER #1: its *name* is *PROVOKING CHANGE*, its *illustration* shows a male warrior dancing with a lightning bolt in his hand, and its QI NUMBER is 27.

These two numbering systems reflect the absolute and relative *qualities of fate* each hexagram bears. The QI NUMBER *is* the hexagram: It is its absolute identity and cannot be divorced from it—it *is* its allotment of *qi* and, therefore, the *quality of fate* it carries. This absolute *quality of fate* expresses itself in the hexagram's *name* and *illustration*. The SEQUENCE NUMBER, on the other hand, defines a hexagram's place in the current arrangement of hexagrams: It depicts its relative identity within the order of the 64 hexagrams—it places it within the continuum of action-and-backlash that makes up the ebb and flow of fate within the realm of life, time and change. This relative *quality of fate* expresses itself in the way that *qi*—whether on the individual or universal level—follows the law of predictable change identified with the current Age (see Intro or Appendix, Why a New I Ching, etc). While people are most often interested in matters of human fortune, every thing, from a star to a thought, has its own *quality of fate* that is represented by its QI NUMBER.

THE CHANGES is, so to speak, the body, whereas *THE ORACLE* is the spirit. Just as it is imperative that we have a thoroughgoing understanding of the body, its instincts, needs and vulnerabilities, it is equally important that we not let those facets of the body drive our decisions, actions, intentions and sense of purpose. The body is not fate and *THE CHANGES* is not predetermination. Just as it is to the invisible half of the body that we turn when we exercise our free will, it is to *THE ORACLE* that we turn when we leap free of predictable change and move at will within the continuum of hexagrams.

```
        #47              #20
      ——— ———          ——— ———
      ———x———          ——————
      ——— ———          ——— ———
      ———⊖———          ——— ———
      ——————           ——— ———
      ———x———          ——————
        39               13
```

In the hypothetical example above, the Oracle responds to a question by identifying our situation within the continuum of hexagrams as SEQUENCE NUMBER #47 *MAKING INDIVIDUAL*.

If there were no line changes in the Oracle's reply, then it would indicate that we were continuing to move along in the sequence from #47 to #48 MOVING SOURCE. This would depict a time in which we were, for better or worse, treading the path of fate without either an opportunity or a need to change course. Such is not the case in the present example, which has line changes in the 1st, 3rd and 5th lines and produces the derived hexagram #20 ENTERING SERVICE. By integrating the Oracle's response into our actions and intentions, we are able to avoid being pulled along by the gravity of predictable cause-and-effect, thereby gaining the freedom to follow the path of good fortune.

We consult *The Oracle* using the coin method, which has since antiquity been called *The Forest of Fire Pearls*. This is the entryway of chance, the means by which *The Oracle* uses *meaningful coincidence* to speak to us of the underlying harmony of all manifestation. By exerting the subtlest influence on the otherwise equal probability of coins falling heads or tails, *The Oracle* makes its intention clear so that we and all others might benefit to the utmost under the present circumstances. The PATTERN OF CHANCE is that of coincidences bound together by the meaningful experience of aware beings: it demonstrates the simultaneity of all events within the single universe of *qi*, allowing us to witness its timeless synchrony as it unpredictably overflows into the timebound world of cause-and-effect. Without chance, the universe would be a static ordering of one predictable cause leading to its inevitable effect, without end. Without *The Oracle*, THE CHANGES would reflect nothing but a predetermined universe without freedom or creativity. With *The Oracle*, THE CHANGES opens the way to inspired thought, inspired feeling, inspired memory and inspired action.

The act of divination is an act of communion between *The Oracle* and the diviner. This is not always apparent at first, of course, because few people take up the practice of divination with the sensitivity to detect the Oracle's presence. It often seems, in the early stage of practice, that one is engaging in a strictly mechanical process of consulting a book of lines and line changes and accompanying interpretation. This perception gives rise to repeated surprise and even epiphanies as the relevance of the Oracle's answers consistently confounds rational explanation. Little by little, however, the diviner's perception shifts from a mechanical process to a living intent: It is at this point that the living presence of the Oracle opens to the diviner's awareness.

The more contact we have with the Oracle the more our thoughts and intentions mirror Its own—the more, in other words, our awareness is attuned to Its own *well of symbols*.

This awakening to the Oracle's *well of symbols* triggers a second shift in our perception, one that awakens the long-dormant *symbol body* within its chrysalis of the personality. As the *constellation of qi* sensitive to the evocative power of symbols, the *symbol body* increasingly subsumes the old personality beneath the immediate appreciation of the symbolic value of all things. Because the *symbol body* perceives the emotional, conceptual and mystical meaning within the Oracle's own *symbol body*, it has also been called the *dream body* and experienced as the bridge between the mortal and immortal bodies. The emergence of the *dream body* is metamorphic: it breaks through the old personality's habitual perceptions and interpretations of self and surroundings, opening up new sensitivities to the sacredness of everything. With familiarity, the personality's inability to penetrate the meaning of symbols is a distant memory.

The act of divination infuses us with a sense of the innate perfectibility of all things, a sense of the inevitable rightness of all things, which brings us into accord with the Oracle's intent and makes the act of reading symbols an act of *recognition of self-sameness*: Our communion with the Oracle brings about a spontaneous identification with the meaning of the Oracle's imagery, which is, ultimately, the imagery of everyday life. The more diviners attune themselves to the Oracle the more they clarify their *qi*, the more they quiet the habit-mind of the personality, and the more they experience the intuitive understanding of the *symbol body*.

9. Everything contains its own contradiction—yet the One is not in any way divided: All dualities are encompassed and resolved in the numinous unity of radiant awareness.

Commentary

This section amplifies the meaning of Section 6, above. The One Mind is a universe of ideas. One of those ideas is *The Many*, the plurality of all things in existence as the opposite of the One Mind. Another of its ideas is *No Mind*, the negation of any duality in existence as the opposite of Mind separate from matter. Even the One Mind, in other words, contains its own contradiction on various levels—how much more so the individual ideas within It. Stepping onto this path of resolved polarities is part and parcel of the cultivation of the *symbol body*.

While there are different ways to describe our experience as humans—either as material beings or spiritual beings or a combination of the two—none of these descriptions offer us the absolute sense of reality that *symbolic beings* does.

73

Setting aside all questions of the reality of matter and spirit, in other words, all we can in fact say about ourselves is that *we are awareness and we interpret whatever we perceive.* We are, in the truest sense, then, *symbolic beings*—and the *symbol body* is our most certain identity in this most uncertain creation within which we find ourselves.

Given that it seems we have a physical body "below" and a nonphysical spirit "above", it is the *symbol body* that stands midway as the true substance of pure awareness and reflective meaning-making. It is for this reason that it is also called the *dream body*, for nothing within its field of awareness can be said with certainty to be other than awareness itself—yet its *being-as-play* treats each object of awareness as a symbol with unknown depths of meaning and meaningfulness.

It is no different than analyzing dreams: the *dream body* is not inspired to investigate the universe of symbols merely by the conceptual meaning of things—it is their emotional meaningfulness that draws us deeper into an awareness of our own emotionally-charged awareness. We can see in our day-to-day dreams that there are no small emotions—nor are there any symbols devoid of meaning. Our *dream body* gleans from the universe of symbols those that are the most meaningful and then arranges them in the most interesting, though not always the most comforting, configurations. This is the aspect of *awareness-as-play* that alludes to the *Sacred Game* within which we play and, almost certainly, are played.

We have to conclude that within the *Sacred Game* of the universe of symbols, which is to say, within the One Mind, we ourselves *are* symbols. On the level of pure awareness, our intrinsic part and participation in the uncreated and imperishable One Mind is that of individual symbols making up the ever-transforming universe of symbols.

At every turn, then, we are faced with a paradoxical *doubling* of awareness that is itself a symbol whose depth of meaningfulness both veils and unveils the emotionally-charged nature of the numinous One. It is *as* symbols within the One Mind that we turn the light of our attention back upon ourselves in a thorough investigation of the mystery of our own meaning and meaningfulness—and it is *as* our *dream body* that that we are able to treat ourselves as another paradoxical symbol to be encompassed and resolved in our own numinous unity.

Chapter VI. *The Way of THE CHANGES*

1. Because all things are One, the more essential a single Idea is, the more purely it reflects the whole. THE CHANGES are comprised solely of a broken or solid line: In this, the most essential form, the whole of creation can be viewed. Conceived at the dawn of consciousness, THE CHANGES reveals the very PATTERN OF PERCEPTION that bonds human being to the WAY of SPIRIT and NATURE. Nothing is beyond its scope because there is nothing that does not share its essence.

Commentary

This section harkens back to the origin of *THE CHANGES,* when consciousness itself took a quantum leap out of the dream-like unconscious state of humanity that had existed until then. At that time, the sages saw their own minds awakening even as many of their contemporaries remained in their sleepwalking state. From this profound experience, the wise women and men posited the metamorphosis of humanity as a direct embodiment of the Great Duality that manifests itself at every level of existence. From this envisioning, it is said, the *essential symbol* was born: a simple line, either broken or unbroken.

This what ties *THE CHANGES* so closely to the Way of Spirit and Nature: It originates from the dawn of consciousness, from that moment which continues to work its numinous power on the human race, for it is nothing less than the evolutionary drive of the One itself as it transmutes the awareness of each being into self-awareness. Such a process mirrors that of the Way of Nature and Spirit, for the transmutation of spirit into matter and matter into soul is the very seedbed of awareness from which human nature blossoms.

If the unbroken line is interpreted as the wall of a fortress and the broken line as its gateway, then the unbroken line symbolizes strength and resistance to vulnerability, whereas the broken line symbolizes openness to relationships and new ideas. If, on the other hand, the unbroken line is interpreted as a clear road ahead and the broken line as an interruption in advancement, then the unbroken line symbolizes ease and progress, whereas the broken line symbolizes rest and waiting before proceeding. In other words, the way in which the broken and unbroken lines are interpreted in their most essential state establishes from the very onset of the meaning-making process the direction the system of symbols will take as a whole. If obsolete cultural values and biases shape the original interpretations of the broken and unbroken lines, then the system of 64 hexagrams—and the Oracle's ability to communicate with us in the current Age—is corrupted.

For this reason, this section explicitly states that the broken and unbroken lines mirror the PATTERN OF PERCEPTION that is indistinguishable from the Way of Nature and Spirit: Because everything is One, human perception can only be made of the same *qi* as all of nature and spirit. The Way of Nature and Spirit, then, is the Way of Human Nature—all that is perceived, in other words, is the same as the perception perceiving it. By beginning with the most fitting interpretations of the broken and unbroken lines, therefore, the system of symbols is coherently attuned to our surroundings, visible and invisible, in a way that links the lifeway of the ancients, the lifeway of our own time, and the intent of the Oracle.

> *2. The solid line symbolizes the masculine half of generative energy: It is the direct action of water, which tunnels through every obstacle on its way to the sea. The broken line symbolizes the feminine half of generative energy: It is the indirect action of water, which nurtures everything it touches as it flows around every obstacle on its way to the sea.*

Commentary

The broken and unbroken lines cannot be interpreted, at their root meanings, as merely abstract concepts. They need to be grounded in real experience that ties nature, human nature and spirit together through their symbology. It is for this reason that the lines link the halves of nature (water), human nature (masculine and feminine) and spirit (generative energy). Grounded in the body, the psyche and the spirit, the symbol of the Great Duality is reflected in the microcosm of the individual lifetime. On the macrocosmic level, the Masculine Creative Force is the universal principle of fire, which inspires all it touches and, within the individual, manifests as the masculine half of the spirit warrior, whereas the Feminine Creative Force is the universal principle of water, which nurtures all it touches and, within the individual, manifests as the feminine half of the spirit warrior.

The overarching symbology of the lines can be seen in the unity of all duality: Water, human nature and spirit all have their two halves but they are still water, human nature and spirit. This is expressed most clearly in the dual nature of water, whose direct, purposeful action channels great canyons from stone and whose indirect, nurturing action brings life to all things. Yet, despite having these two very different natures, water remains water: No one would look at a torrent rushing through stone and a stream meandering through wildflowers and think that these were two different kinds of water—or even two different things altogether, one that carves and one that waters.

It is no different with human nature, of course. Simply because we have two different halves to our nature does not mean there are two different kinds of human beings. Likewise, every individual has a feminine half and a masculine half, regardless of gender.

Out of the nature of the broken and unbroken lines the trigrams are formed. Out of the interaction of the lower and upper trigrams the hexagrams are formed. Out of the system of hexagrams the means of interpreting the Oracle's answers is formed.

> *3. Because THE CHANGES reveals all the possible distributions of generative energy, its hexagrams mirror the sixty-four essential Situations. Because it shows the archetypal constellations of generative energy, its trigrams mirror the cycle of the seasons as they revolve around the eight compass points. Because it reveals the archetypal interchange of masculine and feminine generative energy, its solid and broken lines trace the alternation of the two primal Creative and Sustaining forces. Because it holds sacred the archetypal union of all dualities, it ensures no creation is ever lost.*

Commentary

This section begins by recapitulating the manner in which the system of symbols is constructed, showing how the hexagrams grow out of the trigrams and the trigrams out of the lines. See for example: Book II, Chapter V, Section 7; Book I, Chapter II; and, Sections 1 and 2 of the present Chapter).

Its principle point, though, is that by uniting the Great Duality in its every manifestation, *THE CHANGES* integrates creation and destruction within the *cycle* of *coming and going* (See Figure 17, Book II, Chapter V, Section 6).

This grand cycle of transformation has not even a hair's breadth of a gap through which any creation might ever fall. In the vast indivisible sea of *qi*, not a single drop of matter or spirit is every lost to eternity. On the cosmological level, this is the deeper meaning of *THE CHANGES*: All that has ever existed, or will ever exist, exists in the present moment—it is all the same *qi*, forever evolving through all potential forms and manifestations.

Chapter VII. *The Lessons of THE CHANGES*

1. THE CHANGES teaches that within all things there is an open emptiness, an inner void, that is, Itself, THE WAY. Though the way of the world, the way of Fate, sets a course in the opposite direction, spirit warriors keep their bearings by adhering to this inner compass. Though the way of the world, the way of Fate, presents all the changes of the Age as causes of gain and loss, spirit warriors respond to all the changes of the Age by never stepping outside THE CHANGELESS.

THE CHANGES teaches impeccability by pointing to immortal SPIRIT ennobling everything from within. It teaches authenticity by pointing to mortal NATURE caring for everything from without. Though the way of the world, the way of Fate, fosters competition, spirit warriors collaborate within the nonduality of the living Whole.

Commentary

The primary lesson of *THE CHANGES*, of course, addresses the way to live the most meaningful life. This objective—*the most meaningful life*—is the polestar to which our inner compass ought always point. That it does not always do so and that we often lose our way is attributed to our imposing our limited perspective and personal striving on our relationship between the inner and outer realms. A limited perspective cannot grasp the potential of each moment and personal striving cannot act without aiming for personal advantage: How can trivializing one's life like this lead to the most meaningful life?

For millennia, wise men and women have pointed to the heart-mind that has returned to its original stillness as *THE WAY* to the most meaningful life. Walking such a path, however, brings spirit warriors to the realization that the most meaningful life is the one shared with all. This intention—*that all share in the most meaningful life*—can only be embodied by those who quiet their selfish and fearful thoughts and create an open and inviting heart-mind within which the One might lodge.

Achieving this inner stillness, one finds *THE WAY*, for it is this very clarity of awareness that is utterly attuned to the Whole. The inner void, then, is empty of all the thoughts, emotions and memories that contribute to a limited perspective and personal striving. What is unexpected is that this stillness is *THE WAY* Itself: impossible as it is to imagine ahead of time that the original substance of awareness is nothing other than this stillpoint of Being, such is precisely what we find once we stop the compulsive self-talk of the Thinking mind.

The stillpoint of Being, in which pure awareness flows without fixing upon an object of thought, is *THE CHANGELESS WAY* that carries all toward the most meaningful life as they engage the day-to-day routines of the world of change.

Mimicking Spirit's ennobling influence, spirit warriors do not lapse even for a moment into selfish or fearful thoughts—mimicking Nature's universal generosity, spirit warriors do not lapse even for a moment into selfish or fearful actions. This inability to lapse into habit thoughts and habit actions is called *embodying the lesson of impeccability and authenticity*. Having united the inner and outer realms in a seamless monument of creativity and benevolence, spirit warriors celebrate the universal return to *the most meaningful life* that is the sole intent of the living Whole.

> *2. SPIRIT and NATURE are the invisible and visible halves of the sphere within which change takes place. The inner void of human nature cannot be depleted or extinguished, so it becomes a wellspring of creativity and humaneness. Though the way of the world, the way of Fate, fills people with thoughts, feelings, and memories based on all the changes of the Age, spirit warriors empty their heart-mind of past and future in order to treat each moment impeccably and authentically.*

Commentary

Spirit animates matter, nature materializes spirit. Just as human beings have a visible body and an invisible spirit, so too do all things. Spirit, then, is the invisible half of nature, just as nature is the visible half of spirit. These two halves form a single living Whole whose intention to take form in immanence and yet surmount form in transcendence accounts for all the coming into and going out of this world of birth and death. No amount of learning leads one to direct, first-hand awareness of the One—it is a momentous experience, one of awe and grace, when one breaks through the bounds of Thinking and is suddenly in conscious communion with the World Soul.

Breaking through into Being, weightless within the bottomless depths of uncreated human nature, radiant awareness is conscious light itself, illuminating the vastness of all the hidden mysteries and secret truths of *creative fire* and *humane water*. Not lapsing for even a moment into inattention, spirit warriors preserve the most meaningful life by holding firm to the unspoken lesson of *THE CHANGES*: *Do not trivialize your life*.

Chapter VIII. *On the Text*

1. There is an underlying harmony to the world. It is expressed in the seasons of generative energy, which flows through its patterns into the phenomena of the world. It is of this underlying harmony that the Oracle speaks in the INTENT of each hexagram.

Commentary

Beneath the world of the senses there circulates a vast symphony of *qi* that brings things together and takes things apart based on the principle of *resonance of intent*. Things that will resonate well are brought together, while things that no longer resonate well are taken apart. There is often a notable discrepancy in time frames, however, between things occurring within the underlying harmony and their manifestation in the world of the senses. Because the underlying harmony has its own time, there is often a perceived time lag before its effects are felt in the world of the senses. Less often but just as noteworthy, other effects appear impossibly sudden, manifesting change that would ordinarily take much longer in the world of the senses.

The factors determining resonance are the four seasons of *qi*: Spring-Planting, Summer-Cultivating, Autumn-Harvesting and Winter-Storing (See FIGURE 8: THE INNER COMPASS, Book II, Chapter II, Section 4). Seasons adjacent to one another are said to be resonant, while those opposite one another are said to be dissonant: Intents occupying adjacent seasons are brought together, while intents occupying opposite seasons are taken apart. This bringing together and taking apart embodies the intent of the living Whole, which seeks to harmonize ever higher levels of greater complexity to manifest in the world of the senses as peace and prospering for all.

The text of each hexagram is divided into several parts. Here, the part named INTENT is identified as relevant to the Oracle's furthering the intent of the underlying harmony.

2. There is an underlying purpose to the world. It is expressed in the compass points of generative energy, which circulates like magnetism among everything, attracting to itself the essence of each. It is of this underlying purpose that the Oracle speaks in the ACTION of each hexagram.

Commentary

Beneath the underlying harmony of the world, there circulates a deep-seated and incorruptible thrust of *qi* toward the inevitable perfection of all things. This underlying purpose to Creation is set in motion at the very embodiment of every manifestation of *qi* in the form of a *seed of innate perfectibility*. Each seed of innate perfectibility undergoes a series of *metamorphic instars*, or stages of identity, in an unending progression toward a dynamic and living perfection.

The factors spurring metamorphosis are the four compass points of *qi*: East-Fire, South-Sun, West-Water and North-Moon (See FIGURE 8: THE INNER COMPASS, Book II, Chapter II, Section 4; also, FIGURE 1: THE PRIMAL ARRANGEMENT, Book I, Chapter II, Section 3). From the perspective of the Whole, *the metamorphic purpose constitutes the single action of Creation*—from the perspective of the dead, *the metamorphic purpose constitutes the single action of one's lifetime.*

The text of each hexagram is divided into several parts. Here, the part named ACTION is identified as relevant to the Oracle's furthering the purpose of universal metamorphosis.

> *3. There is an underlying unity to the world. It is expressed in the symbols of generative energy, which unites the dreaming heart-mind with the waking heart-mind. It is of this underlying unity that the Oracle speaks in the INTERPRETATION of each hexagram.*

Commentary

Beneath the underlying purpose of the world, there circulates a fathomless oceanic dream of all possible symbols, all their possible interactions, and all their possible evolutions. This living unity is made up of living parts, the identity of each of which is distinguished by a symbol that represents its specific quality of *qi*. It is an oceanic dream because its symbols are ever emerging out of the deep, moving the waking heart-mind to ever-widening realization.

The factors drawing the unknown into the known are the four turning points of *qi*: Spring Equinox-Initiating Qi, Summer Solstice-Waxing Qi, Autumnal Equinox-Completing Qi and Winter Solstice-Waning Qi (See FIGURE 8: THE INNER COMPASS, Book II, Chapter II, Section 4).

Symbols do not merely emerge into conscious awareness to increase understanding—they also submerge again once their meaning has been incorporated into the lived life. There, in the depths of the Great Mystery they dwell, sometimes for years, acquiring new dimensions of meaning that eventually rise to the surface of knowing when the waking heart-mind is prepared anew.

The text of each hexagram is divided into several parts. Here, the part named INTERPRETATION is identified as relevant to the Oracle's furthering the limitless evolution of realization.

> *4. There is an underlying tide to the world. It is expressed in the waxing and waning of generative energy, which forever raises what is below and lowers what is above. It is of this underlying tide that the Oracle speaks in the LINE CHANGES of each hexagram.*

Commentary

Beneath the underlying unity of the world, there circulates the ebb and flow of *qi* that brings about personal good fortune and misfortune. The confluences of all the currents, counter-currents, eddies, and dams of *qi* produces a maze of possible intents, actions, and interpretations that must be distilled intuitively if the spirit warrior is to make decisions on the spur of the moment. Too many factors exist at any given time for rational analysis to produce optimum good fortune—it is for this reason that *intuitive timing* depends on cultivating a sensitivity to the *kairos*, or magically right moment to act.

The factors contributing to fortunate decisions are the four *kairos* of *qi*: Young Yang-Moderate Light, Old Yang-Extreme Light, Young Yin-Moderate Dark and Old Yin-Extreme Dark (See FIGURE 8: THE INNER COMPASS, Book II, Chapter II, Section 4). Knowing when to wait and when to act are as important as knowing what action to take. For this reason, *intuitive timing* remains vigilant to incipient fluctuations of *qi* that have not yet crossed the threshold of change: sensing that times of stability are changing and that times of change are stabilizing allows spirit warriors to arrive at decision points alongside *kairos*.

The text of each hexagram is divided into several parts. Here, the part named LINE CHANGES is identified as relevant to the Oracle's furthering good fortune. The following examples demonstrate the manner in which the Oracle advises, warns and informs in order to further good fortune and avoid misfortune.

5. *"The purity of a parent—you cannot but fulfill your responsibilities to those who depend on you. Nonetheless, you are loved for who you are and not for what you do—you are most fortunate to be accepted by those close to you. Keep the mutual concern circulating among you."*

Commentary

This quote is of the Second Line Change in Hexagram #8 HARMONIZING DUALITY. It is a solid line changing into a broken line. It refers to the issue of Trust and Bonding (See Figure 9: THE SIX STAGES OF THE HEXAGRAM, Book II, Chapter 3, Section 3).

It is not always possible to strike a harmonious balance between our roles and relationships but this line change denotes a particularly favorable time to do just that. Here one's sense of duty is so ingrained that there is never any question of fulfilling one's responsibilities—that this is noteworthy, however, implies that matters are not entirely simple or easy and that others might withdraw from the pressure. One's loyalty, though, becomes as appreciated as any of one's actions and those one serves exhibit the genuine affection they feel—not just gratitude but deep-seated caring. The mutual devotion cements an alliance that can only come undone if feelings of mutual trust and respect are not honored and cultivated by all.

6. *"The bond between above and below is unbreakable, forged in the fires of many shared trials and tribulations. You can count on this relationship to the end—just as the union of man and woman produces a child, you are producing something that will outlast you. Radiate the peace you feel."*

Commentary

This quote is of the Fifth Line Change in Hexagram #62 CONCEIVING SPIRIT. It is a solid line changing into a broken line. It refers to the issue of Authority and Empowerment (See Figure 9: THE SIX STAGES OF THE HEXAGRAM, Book II, Chapter 3, Section 3).

This is a significant line change coming at the culmination of the process of self-realization. Occurring in the place of empowerment in the sixty-second hexagram, it speaks of the final stages of the inner alchemical process. The upper, celestial, spirit is fully fused with the lower, earthly, spirit and their fixity produces the immortal spirit body during one's own lifetime.

Fear disappears, time disappears, shadow disappears: It is incumbent upon one to embody and exhibit the serenity and joyousness that comes with completing the work. The goal of self-realization is never self-realization itself, after all, but the full and efficacious incarnation of the creative principle at play in this glorious world of worlds.

Beyond the esoteric reading, this line change marks a relationship between two people of similar spirit, one older and one younger, one a teacher and one a student. This situation is highly beneficial for both, keeping the elder's work alive and setting the younger's feet firmly upon the living path. Those with a full belly are not hungry: having found one's way, there is no more seeking. Waiting beside the river, all the water one could ever need flows one's way.

> 7. "*Cautious to the point of being timid, accommodating to the point of being conciliatory—this serves well enough for now but you will need to be more decisive and purposeful in the time ahead. The kind of confidence that is needed cannot by faked, however. Build on your real strengths.*"

Commentary

This quote is of the First Line Change in Hexagram #7 COMPELLING MOTIVE. It is a broken line changing into a solid line. It refers to the issue of Vulnerability and Dependence (See Figure 9: THE SIX STAGES OF THE HEXAGRAM, Book II, Chapter 3, Section 3).

One cannot stand in the doorway forever—sooner or later, one must enter the room. One cannot remain at the beginning forever—sooner or later, one must enter a higher level of play and engage a higher level of players. This is a line change warning one of the need to cultivate a different sense of self in order to meet change head-on: It cannot be a contrived demeanor, though, and so needs to be grounded in those facets of one's character and experience that bring with them a stronger sense of inner strength and outer flexibility. A more demanding time awaits one ahead, one that demands a strong sense of purpose and ability to adjust to change decisively and spontaneously. The advice focuses on the concept of transferable skills, taking what one already knows intimately and transferring those lessons and strategies to another, more sophisticated, field of action.

> 8. "*Believe in those around you, support their efforts, and encourage them when times are trying. When they see how this attitude results in your own accomplishments, their confidence will be renewed and they will redouble their efforts Use your strengths to bolster others from below.*"

Commentary

This quote is of the Third Line Change in Hexagram #49 STAYING OPEN. It is a solid line changing into a broken line. It refers to the issue of Separation and Alienation (See Figure 9: THE SIX STAGES OF THE HEXAGRAM, Book II, Chapter 3, Section 3).

Sometimes the position of outsider can be used provide others an example of alternative approaches to life's difficulties. In the present situation, the Oracle advises one to work from a position of humility, supporting others without drawing attention to one's own strengths. It is often the case that people who share a particular view cannot recognize the value of those who see things differently. It is pointless to take this personally. When one is moving through a situation, it is best to encourage the best in others and not to criticize their ways or belittle their beliefs. Be of benefit wherever you go and you will always be welcome back.

> 9. *"When the imaginative power wanes, stop producing new work. Return to the origins of your vision and rework them in light of what you know now. Do not listen to others appealing to your vanity for their own self-interest."*

Commentary

This quote is of the Sixth Line Change in Hexagram #51 LIVING ESSENCE. It is a solid line changing into a broken line. It refers to the issue of Interdependence and Wisdom (See Figure 9: THE SIX STAGES OF THE HEXAGRAM, Book II, Chapter 3, Section 3).

The yang energy of the pioneer and explorer does not last forever. When the yang energy wanes, be prepared to shift into the yin energy of the midwife, who brings new things fully into the world. This line change is a warning to know when to pull back from energetic advancement in order to consolidate inner power and complete outer accomplishments. It especially advises one to revise previous work and ideas from the standpoint of a more mature and knowledgeable perspective. In such a time of tying up loose ends, it is essential to remain true to one's vision and not get pulled off track by the whims of others, no matter how enticingly they appeal to one's sense of self-importance. The question here is *How do I wish to be remembered?*

10. *"Just because you can do something doesn't mean you should—to humble others is seldom wise. Keep your thoughts to yourself and use your talents to build others up. These matters are not essential to you, so stop being so invested in them and help others around you succeed."*

Commentary

This quote is of the First Line Change in Hexagram #20 ENTERING SERVICE. It is a solid line changing into a broken line. It refers to the issue of Dependence and Vulnerability (See Figure 9: THE SIX STAGES OF THE HEXAGRAM, Book II, Chapter 3, Section 3).

To humble oneself is wisdom, to humble another is folly. To expect people to fully appreciate one's help is an extravagance of self-importance and has no place in a life of service. This is a line change advising one to keep both feet on the path of compassion. Serving others is itself the highest calling and an end in itself. To place all others above us *without us changing in any way* is a lifeway that ennobles all. We must, moreover, be ever wary to not become dependent on those we serve for our sense of identity. What they do with our gifts is a matter of their own will and judgment—if gifts are given with strings attached, then they are fish hooks and not gifts at all.

11. *"In the course of performing your duties, you repeatedly exaggerate the importance of your position. You have neither the strength nor backing to hold on to it, however, so now others can take it away from you if they want it. Before you speak or act, ask yourself, what can go wrong?"*

Commentary

This quote is of the Third Line Change in Hexagram #44 REFINING INSTINCT. It is a broken line changing into a solid line. It refers to the issue of Separation and Alienation (See Figure 9: THE SIX STAGES OF THE HEXAGRAM, Book II, Chapter 3, Section 3).

The third line is typically in a difficult position and here, in the situation of REFINING INSTINCT, it finds itself out of place entirely. The instinct toward an alpha-position within the social group must be reined in before it becomes irreversibly self-defeating. This line change is a strong warning to stop acting heedlessly. Too much inattentiveness to how others are responding to one is about to result in unexpected loss and separation.

The Oracle's advice is to think ahead more than just one move at a time, recognizing that many of those around you are more skilled players than yourself. If you intend to stay with this endeavor, slow down and learn the unspoken rules of conduct. At the very least, the lesson of not exaggerating one's importance should be incorporated into one's attitude and behavior.

Chapter IX. *On the Oracle*

1. The number of a broken line is 8, the number of a solid line is 7. The number of a broken line changing into a solid line is 6, the number of a solid line changing into a broken line is 9.

Commentary

This and the following sections explain in detail the mediumistic basis for the Oracle's ability to communicate with diviners (see Book I, Chapter I). Here, the basic mechanism symbolizing change in the real world is laid out. The numbers 6, 7, 8 and 9 represent the four kinds of lines that express the four fundamental kinds of change, which are thought of as qualities of *qi* in its form as acting (7), waiting (8), acting shifting to waiting (9) and waiting shifting to acting (6).

These symbols are neither narrow nor shallow.

Acting connotes purposeful action toward a goal. But it also connotes a specific type of action—one that is responsive to circumstances, one that seeks the best for all concerned, and one that is spontaneous and uncontrived. It connotes, in other words, *inspired action*, the expression of *magnanimous qi* that is routinely cultivated and stored up for just such actions. Because acting is a response to *need*, it must be executed with particular sensitivity to both the timing of one's action and the possibility of one's action creating negative backlashes. For this reason, *acting* is oftentimes associated with *wisdom*.

Waiting connotes just that space of time between inspired action when *magnanimous qi* is taken in, cultivated and stored up until it is needed. While there exist many methods of gathering in *qi*, they all have as their basis a heart-mind that is open, calm, quiet and welcoming. The goal of enlightened practice is *not* to gather in *qi* in quiet sitting—the goal is to gather in *qi* when walking or sitting, standing up or lying down. It is, in other words, *routinely cultivated*, part of a methodology that does not rely on any formalized practice—it is a matter of attuning oneself to the *feeling* of magnanimous *qi* and remaining open to it, making a lodging place for it, distilling it down to its essence, and holding it fast until the time comes to release it in inspired action. Because waiting is based on collecting *magnanimous qi*, it is oftentimes associated with *compassion*.

From one perspective, *acting* is the dynamic expression of *qi* as the apt and unexpected response to circumstances—hence its association with the *creative principle*. Likewise, *waiting* is the self-contained accumulation of *qi* as the universally beneficial embracing of circumstances—hence its association with the *receptive principle*.

From another perspective, *acting* is the natural, appropriate, and spontaneous catalyst of creation, whereby all things are inspired to take form and strive toward continual metamorphosis—hence its association with the *masculine creative force*. Similarly, *waiting* is the natural, appropriate, and spontaneous benevolence of creation, whereby all thing are accorded an equal measure of essential benefit—hence its association with the *feminine creative force*.

Over the course of time, *acting* comes to the end of usefulness and must shift into *waiting*. And, of course, over time, *waiting* come to the end of preparation and must shift into *acting*. Seen in this way, *waiting* is a particular stage of change that sustains the status quo in order to gather strength for the leap ahead, while *acting* is that stage of change that upsets the status quo in order to evoke a more positive equilibrium. The over-arching relationships between the four states of change can best be envisioned as those of the four seasons (See FIGURE 8: THE INNER COMPASS, Book II, Chapter II, Section 4).

> *2. Invoking the Forest of Fire Pearls method, use three coins to consult the Oracle, counting the head side as 3 and the tail side as 2.*

Commentary

The *Forest of Fire Pearls* is the ancient name of the coin method of consulting the Oracle. As one addresses the Oracle with a question, it is especially beneficial to invoke the name of the mediumistic channel, which establishes a heart-mind connection reaching back to the very origins of the Oracle's relationship with human beings.

As for the mechanics of a consultation, there are only four possible results of each throw of three coins—

Three Tails =	$2 + 2 + 2 = 6$
Two Tails & One Heads =	$2 + 2 + 3 = 7$
Two Heads & One Tails =	$3 + 3 + 2 = 8$
Three Heads =	$3 + 3 + 3 = 9$

3. Throw the coins six times in order to determine the six lines of the hexagram. The total of the first throw of the coins counts as the bottom line, the total of the last throw of the coins counts as the top line.

Commentary

The Oracle replies to our consultation by speaking through the hexagrams. Throwing the coins six times results in the six lines of a hexagram. Like a plant growing from the ground up, hexagrams are built from the bottom, up: The first line of each hexagram is at the bottom and the sixth line of the hexagram is at the top.

4. Totaling the three coins for each throw results in either a 6, a 7, an 8, or a 9.

Commentary

Each of the six throws is totaled and its results are then translated into one of the four lines.

5. Two tails and one heads totals 7, which is the number of a solid line. Two heads and one tails totals 8, which is the number of a broken line.

Commentary

The unchanging lines are drawn thus:

   7 = ————————   8 = —— ——

6. Three tails totals 6, which is the number of a changing broken line, three heads totals 9, which is the number of a changing solid line. A 6 changes into a 7, a 9 changes into an 8.

Commentary

The changing lines are drawn thus:

   6 = ——x——   9 = ——ө——

7. The first three throws result in the lower, or inner, trigram. The second three throws result in the upper, or outer, trigram.

Commentary

Even though the Oracle speaks in hexagrams, its parts of speech are the trigrams making up the hexagrams. The lower trigram represents the inner nature of a person, institution or situation, while the upper trigram represents the outer nature of a person, institution or situation. The trigrammic interaction of inner and outer natures is what shapes the nature and meaning of their respective hexagram.

> *8. Each of the 64 hexagrams can, through the combination of line changes, turn into any one of the other 63 hexagrams. Because such combinations of line changes include the possibility of no line changes, the actual number of possible permutations among the hexagrams is the square of 64, or 4,096.*

Commentary

The concern of this section is not strictly mathematical. Its point is that the odds of receiving any given reading from the Oracle are *not* 1 in 64—rather, they are 1 in 4,096. This is because the Oracle speaks in "complete sentences". Its reply always addresses the situation as its has developed to this point *and* the situation as it is developing into the next space of time—it always addresses the present situation and the future developing out of it, in other words.

The first, or present, hexagram in the Oracle's reply generally contains some combination of line changes. In the example below, Hexagram #1 PROVOKING CHANGE has two line changes, a 9 in the first, or bottom, line and a 6 in the fifth line. When these two lines change into their respective opposites—*all the lines with values of 7 or 8 remaining unchanged*—the second, or future, hexagram is produced (in this example, Hexagram #19 CELEBRATING PASSAGE).

Working from the bottom, up in the example below—

> the solid line in the first place changes to a broken line
>
> the broken line in the second place does not change
>
> the broken line in the third place does not change
>
> the solid line in the fourth place does not change
>
> the broken line in the fifth place changes to a solid line
>
> the broken line in the sixth place does not change

```
         #1                    #19
    ——— ———            ——— ———
    ———x———            ——————
    ——————            ——————
    ——— ———            ——— ———
    ——— ———            ——— ———
    ———Θ———            ——— ———
```

This is the power of the four lines (6, 7, 8 and 9). *This* is the secret way that the Oracle has been able, through the millennia, to teach human nature to be ever more aware of incipient trends within their surroundings and their foreseeable consequences. *This* mechanism, by which the four lines combine with the six places, is what allows us to analyze the elements of change and stability in our surroundings and to make decisions that take us from the path of fate to the path of freedom. (See Figures 10 and 11, Book II, Chapter II, Section 3).

There are 63 different possible combinations of line changes in any given hexagram. That means that any given hexagram can change into 63 different hexagrams. There is, additionally, the possibility that a hexagram contains all sevens and eights, so it does not change into another hexagram. This possibility, that a hexagram doesn't change, raises the number of future hexagrams that can develop from the present one to 64. For this reason, the odds of receiving any given reply from the Oracle are 1 in 4,096.

In cases where a hexagram contains no line changes, it does not mean that the situation is not changing. Rather, it means that one is in the flow of the sequence of hexagrams—that the future hexagram is the next in the arrangement of the 64 hexagrams. For example, if the Oracle's reply was Hexagram #1 PROVOKING CHANGE, with no line changes, then the future situation would be Hexagram #2 SENSING CREATION. In such cases, it is not necessary to read the text for any line changes, since the Oracle is saying (following the example) that the forces preserving the momentum and direction within PROVOKING CHANGE lead naturally into SENSING CREATION.

For all the reasons above, it is clear that a full reading of the Oracle's answer must take into account not just the changing lines but the unchanging lines, as well. After all, the developing situation owes just as much to the forces preserving the status quo (the unchanging lines) as it does the forces transforming specific stages within the situation (the changing lines). There are traditions in the past that emphasized the *unchanging* lines over the changing lines, so it is incumbent upon contemporary diviners to recognize the equal value the Oracle places on the forces driving metamorphosis and the forces preserving the status quo (See FIGURE 12: MARKING SHIFTS OF ATTENTION, Book II, Chapter II, Section 5).

———

See also Volume I of this series, *I Ching Mathematics: The Science of Change*.

9. The Oracle reveals the path of Fate and points to the path of Freedom. With its help, spirit warriors respond to events without self-interest, thereby helping to bring the Creative Forces' vision closer to realization.

Commentary

The sequence of 64 hexagrams demonstrates the predictable backlashes to change in the current Age. This is called the *path of fate* in the sense that everything born grows old, its *qi* leaks out, and it dies. It is fate in the sense of a predictable entropic process of progressive deterioration and dissolution. This entropic process is not restricted to living beings, of course. We can see it at work in the development of social institutions as much as in the workings of the physical nature of the universe.

The Oracle, through the use of the line changes, illumines the *path of freedom* by showing us the decision points that can pull us out of the *sequence of hexagrams*. This it does by drawing our attention to the archetypal elements within the present hexagram and how they are developing into a future hexagram that does not follow the *sequence of hexagrams*. In the example in section 8, above, for instance, Hexagram #1 PROVOKING CHANGE changes into Hexagram #19 CELEBRATING PASSAGE instead of following the *sequence of hexagrams* to Hexagram #2 SENSING CREATION. (See Book I, Chapter II).

For human nature, the *path of fate* is governed by the force of self-interest, for that is what sets its own entropic process in motion. The Oracle teaches that the path of good fortune lies in stepping off the *path of fate* and back into one's own essential nature, which seeks the best for all at the same time. By attuning themselves to the intent of the Creative Forces in this manner, spirit warriors add their own intent to the momentum of the great perfecting spirit upholding the whole of Creation. By studying the sequence of 64 hexagrams making up the *path of fate*, spirit warriors sensitize themselves to the predictable unfolding of events governed by the law of spiritual cause-and-effect.

10. The Oracle teaches the Way Forward and the Way Backward so that spirit warriors might both explore to the utmost and return to the centermost.

<u>Commentary</u>

This saying is a highly esoteric formula relating to the evolution of the soul. The Way Forward is the furthermost distance one explores—through a combination of effort, curiosity and allies—of the spiritual landscape. The Way Backward is the unimpeded return—through a combination of joyousness, nonresistance and gratitude—to the Origin. It is understood here that the Way Forward takes one further and further from the Origin, accounting for the varying degrees of wakefulness among contemporaries. Those souls who stay too close to the Origin, whether out of love or fear, fail to realize their full potential of awareness. Those souls who press ever outward from the Origin, whether out of passion or self-sacrifice, break through wall after wall of sleep, awakening ever-deeper dimensions of awareness. This bringing to light the deepest mysteries of creation furthers the purpose, and is in perfect accord with the intent, of the Origin.

The Oracle teaches this lesson of *going out and coming in* by means of the *path of freedom*, which is to say, by means of hexagrams changing into one another outside the *sequence of hexagrams*. This is nowhere more apparent than in the binary sequence of the hexagrams, which begins with LIVING ESSENCE and ends with DAWNING EXISTENCE (See FIGURE 18: THE FU XI ARRANGEMENT OF THE HEXAGRAMS, Book II, Part I, Chapter 5, Section 8). Here, the Origin is understood as the living essence of infinite potential out of which all things are born—and the furthermost reach being the ever-dawning existence of infinite diversity that is the realization of potential. When the binary number of the first hexagram is less than its derived hexagram, then the movement is toward Dawning Existence, or the Way Forward. Contrariwise, if the first hexagram's binary number is greater than its derived hexagram's, then the movement is toward Living Essence, or the Way Backward. (See n/a: MATHEMATICS OF QI {yet to be written})

Chapter X. *THE CHANGES as Spirit Ally*

1. THE CHANGES accompany spirit warriors on their journey through lifetimes. In formulating words, we ought to learn its lessons. In making decisions, we ought to reflect on its changes. In conceiving endeavors, we ought to adopt its point of view. In understanding the future, we ought to empty our mind to make a place for the Oracle to lodge.

2. Because there is but One Mind, spirit warriors do not have to make their thoughts and feelings known in words—we concentrate on the matter at hand, looking at it from different viewpoints, so that the Oracle can feel our intent and place it within the intent of THE ONE. Because all of creation is but one moment, there is neither distance in place nor time in the Oracle's view—it answers our needs like a valley's echo, like a mirror's reflection, showing us the direction of change within the ocean of THE CHANGELESS.

Commentary

What is most difficult for us to keep in mind on a day-to-day basis is that we are immortal beings. Deathless in passing through the ordeal of mortality, courageous in passing through the ordeal of grief, wise in passing through the ordeal of change, loving in passing through the ordeal of individuality—the lessons of the embodied soul enrich the Whole and ennoble the lived life of the spirit warrior. The fact one is drawn to THE CHANGES in this lifetime is a strong indication that it has played an important part in one's previous lifetimes—that it is a spirit ally that accompanies one throughout this life of lifetimes.

This section reminds us that words are the act of naming things, the act of speaking symbols, and that we ought to respect the depth of wisdom vested in THE CHANGES and open ourselves to the life lessons its symbols contain. Such lessons, especially those centered around inspired action within changing circumstances, ennoble our intentions and clarify our decisions. As volition continues to manifest outwardly, decisions lead to initiating endeavors that effect our surroundings, so it behooves us to take up the ancient heart-mind of universal benefit espoused by THE CHANGES. Moving further outward yet, awareness stands before the Gate of Coming and Going, watching incipient change taking form as it seeks to leave the future and enter the present—in this way, diviners mirror the very mind of the Oracle.

Focusing on a specific question to the exclusion of all others is not the way to consult the Oracle. Believing that a question must be spoken aloud is not the way to approach the Oracle. Because every matter has more than one perspective from which it can be viewed, it is important to open up one's question to as many points of view as one can imagine. Because every question has an emotional element, it should be part of one's concentrated attention when consulting the Oracle. Because the coins, one's question, and the Oracle all exist together in the same ocean of timeless *qi*, it is the diviner's reverential attitude and sincere intention that aligns with THE ONE, thereby eliciting the most meaningful answer.

3. Casting the Oracle, we build up the hexagram line by line. If the count is 7, then it is a solid line that does not change. If the count is 8, then it is a broken line that does not change. If the count is 9, then it is a solid line that changes into a broken line. If the count is 6, then it is a broken line that changes into a solid line. When the Oracle's answer contains any line changes, then a second hexagram is formed in order to show the coming Season. In the space before the Oracle is cast, all the permutations among the hexagrams are held in potential—in the space after the Oracle has been cast, its answer has been narrowed down to just one among the possible four thousand.

Commentary

This section essentially reiterates the divinatory mechanism presented in Chapter 9, above, and is part of the cumulative instruction commending the teachings to memory.

4. THE CHANGES has no awareness—but the Oracle does. The lines and trigrams and hexagrams are emblems, symbols, of the way in which generative energy flows through all things—the emblems without the Oracle would be like a corpse after the spirit has left. We approach the Oracle with a sense of reverence and exploration, thereby inducing it to move the lines of its body in answering our question.

Commentary

The Oracle is the *Speaking* of the One Mind, the radiant awareness standing outside the flow of time yet in communion with timebound human nature. The lines do move nor do they speak but as activated and given voice by the Oracle. Without an intuitive grasp of the living awareness within all form—and without a sense of the sacredness of both—how can one be called a spirit warrior? how can one be called a diviner?

5. THE CHANGES allows spirit warriors to break down the barrier between themselves and the world, thereby returning to THE ONE and uniting SPIRIT and NATURE.

6. How can we call allies to us if we do not make ourselves receptive to their own intentions? How can we arrive at the juncture ahead of time if we do not make ourselves sensitive to the initial seeds of change? How can we not be sacred if everything is?

<u>Commentary</u>

THE CHANGES shows us the archetypal forces of nature around us, as well as the archetypal forces of spirit within us. By showing us how our inner nature is identical to our outer nature, THE CHANGES makes evident our indivisibility with THE ONE. The heart-mind of spirit warriors is a vast unnamed expanse without any artificial barrier marring the free circulation of unifying awareness. As the alchemical marriage of nature and spirit, THE CHANGES produces in the spirit warrior a second body—the intentional body, the dream body, the symbol body, the diamond body, the immortal spirit body—that is utterly one with the mystical power of all Creation.

When we think only of the help that we need, we significantly reduce the number of potential allies we might find. When we think of all the ways we might be of help to allies in the realization of their own vision, we significantly increase the number of potential allies we might find. *Mutual benefit* is the basis of forging alliances. When it comes to matters of timing and stepping onto the path of good fortune, the basis is *universal benefit*—taking up the nature of water, which nourishes everything it touches, we train ourselves to become increasingly aware of the incipient seeds of *qi* about to break the surface of manifestation. As we treat all around us as sacred in this way, we cannot help but come to the realization that we ourselves are sacred, as well—it is the inevitable result of spirit warriors' transformation that they move with the nobility of sacred beings within the sacred space they share with all other sacred beings.

7. It is by our impeccable sincerity that we forge an unbreakable bond with the Oracle and are accompanied by it on our journey through lifetimes.

<u>Commentary</u>

Essence recognizes essence: those drawn to THE CHANGES remember it from other times. It is a spirit ally whose charisma—whose spiritual power—informs all within its alliance, imbuing each with its individual allotment of the *qi* of THE WAY. The diviner recognizes the Oracle: the Oracle recognizes the diviner.

Chapter XI. *The Language of the Oracle*

1. THE CHANGES reveal the ending and beginning of things amid the temporary continuity of other things. By moving with the timing of the cycles of change, spirit warriors extend their intentions out to harmonize all others'. In this way, they come to understand where they need to apply their energies at each point in this lifetime.

Commentary

The secret Way of Change is the *Way of Endings*. To understand THE CHANGES and be guided by its wisdom along the path of good fortune, it is necessary to pull one's eyes away from the dramas and promises of the beginning of things and focus instead on the creative and beneficial endings of things. Things are small and easy to direct when they begin but strong and willful when they end—if one does not enter into each matter with an intent to bring it to completion in the most beneficial manner possible, then the ensuing beginnings one enters into will continue to betoken melodrama and unfulfilled promise. It is not a matter of having a goal or destination in mind at the beginning. Indeed, it is completely contrary to such a practice, since it runs counter to the spirit of exploration and creative expression. Water has a purpose—to follow gravity until it reaches the sea—but it is the most adaptable of things, flowing around and under and through everything in its path of least resistance. For spirit warriors, the purpose is to benefit all things at the same time. However, the way in which this is achieved in each instance cannot be predicted ahead of time. Purpose is not the same thing as goal, just as strategy is not the same thing as tactics. One cannot *plan* an ending but it is possible to *intend* what kind of ending best expresses magnanimous *qi*.

Counterintuitive as it may seem, focusing on the ending of things charges each new beginning with a kind of mythical presence, a kind of symbolic behavior, that builds momentum even as direction shifts along the line of least resistance in between. This direction of events between beginning and ending is what most people attend to, believing them to be more controllable than beginnings and endings, which seem driven primarily by the momentum of circumstances. The reality, however, is far different. It is the *temporary continuity* of things that is primarily driven by the momentum of circumstances, whereas beginnings can be increasingly influenced by applying the greatest focus to endings. In practice, this is accomplished by *treating each moment as an ending.*

In this sense, it can be said that the Oracle speaks in a metaphorical language of endings. It teaches us to constantly attend to the imminent end of things, to keep our awareness centered on the ethics of inspired behavior, treating each person, animal, plant, natural phenomenon and spirit as a sacred being reflective of the same light we ourselves reflect. Spirit warriors treat all they encounter with this kind of impeccable sincerity because it is the surest way to defeat the self-defeating thoughts, emotions and memories that lead to a trivialized life. Since ancient times, this lifeway has been called *Flower and Song*, a difrasismo meaning *poetry* in the sense of a *poetic participation in life*. The *Flower* part of this metaphor draws our attention to the perfection of the blossoming flower—and the fact that the blossom is dying right before our eyes. This symbol of the flower is extended to all existence. Everything is in this instant perfect and passing away. Everything we know and love, in other words, is in the moment absolutely perfect as it is—and moving inexorably toward death. Holding both this awe of perfection and this grief at its loss together in the conscious heart-mind is something only a spirit warrior can do authentically. To live authentically, it is said, means walking with this sense of joyous awe and heartbreaking grief as one encounters every moment. In this way, we are the most awake to the truth and beauty and mystery of living. The *Song* part of the metaphor means that to live authentically also means that this truth of *Flower* must be spoken, must be expressed, must be embodied in every act if we are to honor the Creative Forces and all that comes into manifestation within this glorious Creation and inevitably departs. Together, *Flower and Song* means that the mythic life, the most meaningful life, the non-trivialized life, is found in encountering each person, place, and thing as it stands eternal in the moment—blossoming out of the Invisible and fading back into it simultaneously—and engaging each with the honor, respect, and cordiality accorded every reflection of THE ONE. This is the origin of sayings like *Keep death as an adviser*.

The *continuity of things* in this sense can be misleading—unduly attending to it can trick one into treating things as if they will endure forever and, consequently, into taking them for granted. The way of the trivialized life lies along such a path of inattention and disregard. It encourages us to see things as not-yet-perfect and needing to progress toward our own concept of betterment. And it lulls us into the sleep of not treating things with the compassion they deserve for facing death in this world of mortality.

In the same way that having one's first child brings an end to one's own childhood, Spring brings an end to Winter. And, just as disaster befalls those who do not end their own childhood once they have a child of their own, those who do not recognize that Winter has ended will not take up the Spring plow and sowing that makes for the harvest's riches. Farmers sensing the cycling current of life ebbing and flowing beneath the surface of appearances are no different than enlightened parents who sense the profound honor bestowed upon them in being entrusted with the sacred duty of ennobling the heart-mind of the newest addition to the great cycling current of life ebbing and flowing beneath the surface of the generations.

It is not just the birth of a new child that marks the ending of a previous way of life—every moment marks the end of a previous sense of self, the end of a previous identification with habitual thoughts, emotions, and memories, the end of another chapter of one's personal history. Rather than aiming at starting things or keeping things going, spirit warriors make it a practice to aim at ending things—at ending this part of one's behavior in a relationship, at ending one's tendency toward melancholia, at ending one's need for attention or acceptance, at ending one's participation in an endeavor, at ending one's frustration with society, at ending one's sense of something missing in one's life. By this practice of concentrating their attention on ending the right things in the right way, spirit warriors enter each moment with the freedom to pivot at will, dropping off every encumbrance to apt and unexpected responses to circumstances as they arise.

2. THE CHANGES teach that sooner or later, everything changes into its opposite. Just as the sunny side of a mountain in the morning becomes the shaded side in the afternoon, with time every change provokes a backlash. The line changes point to the timing of decisions and the values upon which those decisions are based.

Grounding their actions in the ethics of benefiting the Whole, spirit warriors abandon self-interest, seek neither fame nor recognition, and cultivate their inner power in private. They seek to dampen the self-destructive tendencies in civilization by building alliances based on compassion and wisdom. They repair the past through the judicious practice of the Art of Starting Over.

Commentary

The Oracle speaks in the language of endings because without endings there is no change.

This is especially true on the grand scale of humanity, whose collective unconscious cannot shift into the next Age without ending its exploration of the darker side of human nature. Only after it has cornered itself through its pursuit of individual and group dominance, trapping itself in a living nightmare of self-destruction from which there is no waking, does it spontaneously accept that the inevitable end has arrived and so welcome the Age of peace and prospering for all. This eventual positive backlash of the collective unconscious is part of the deep structure of the Oracle's language. The hexagrams move from #64 SAFEGUARDING LIFE to #1 PROVOKING CHANGE and then all the way back to #64 SAFEGUARDING LIFE, in a five thousand year cycle of human metamorphosis. Since ancient times, the Oracle's language has embodied the *Universal Civilizing Spirit*, the most coherent radiant awareness that consistently exerts its subtle influence to awaken the individual and collective unconscious from their sleepwalking state. The *walls of sleep* form a progressive set of barriers holding individuals and groups back from awakening to their full embodiment of magnanimous *qi*.

The Oracle speaks in the language of endings because without endings there is no starting over. Ending things in the right way at the right time brings about mutual understanding, forgiveness, and reconciliation—all precursors to a new beginning of building trust, acceptance, and mutual benefit. So long as the past remains an *object of continuity*, ingrained thoughts, emotions and memories keep surfacing to prolong division, discord and distress. The *Art of Starting Over* is one of feelings—it is an emotional backlash to the prospect of remaining stuck in a living nightmare forever. Its *art* lies in triggering the most meaningful ending possible and then riding out the repercussions as the new equilibrium asserts itself.

> *3. THE WAY is cyclic, ever returning to the mysterious origin. Spirit warriors develop new senses in order to follow THE WAY back to the ACT OF CREATION. Reuniting THE ONE and THE MANY within themselves, they see the way to end things and begin them anew. In accord with the intent of THE WAY, they help the obsolete and exhausted change into their opposite. Who but those who practice mental fasting can facilitate change without setting in motion a negative backlash?*

Commentary

Because THE WAY is cyclic, the way forward, when followed to its furthermost point, is the way back—the destination of all things is ultimately the same homeland. The same longing occupies all souls, the same vague feeling just beyond the pale of memory haunts every wayfarer on this pilgrimage of lifetimes.

It is the soulic equivalent of fish spawning and birds migrating back to their birthplace—it is the spiritual *instinct of return*, triggered by the soul's ineffable sense of homesickness. An unremembered Origin calls from the depths of pure oblivion and we ache to answer as the turns of the labyrinth carry us further toward an unremembered Destination. There is no place for timidity on the soul's journey—it needs to be undertaken in the spirit of adventure and curiosity and daring.

The five senses are not enough on this pilgrimage. They cannot tell us about the underlying harmony of *qi*, the permutations of which make up this world of the five senses. It is for this reason that spirit warriors turn to the eight trigrams, recognizing in them the means of sensing the subsensorial circulation of *qi* as it works its way into manifestation. Finding these eight archetypes of *qi* within themselves, spirit warriors discover their sudden attunement to *all* the manifestations of *qi* everywhere. It is in this sense that the trigrams become the new senses of the spirit warrior (See Book II, Chapter 4, Section 3).

As this attunement to the eight archetypes of *generative energy* becomes the primary experience of conscious awareness, our heart-minds are less and less preoccupied with trivial habits of thought, emotion and memory. It is as if the sun and moon, wind and lightning, fire and water, mountain and lake, all moved into our inner landscape: The light of day and the light of night, the sound of the wind and the rolling thunder, the warmth of fire and the coolness of the stream, the height of the mountain and the depth of the lake—what thought is there? Called since ancient times, *mental fasting*, our return to radiant awareness is completely aligned with the intent of THE ONE and so introduces no friction or resistance into the field of intentions that might cause a negative backlash.

> *4. Therefore they call a broken rung Stillness and a solid rung Movement. Repairing a broken rung or breaking a solid rung they call Change. Ascending and descending without end they call Journeying. What shows itself behind the eyes they call Dreaming. Eradicating that which takes root in the body they call Stalking. That which organizes change they call Habit. That which benefits all by ascending and descending they call the Creative and Sustaining Forces.*

Commentary

Here the hexagrams are envisioned as ladders and the lines as rungs. A broken rung (8) is called Stillness because it halts ascent or descent. A solid rung (7) is called Movement because it permits ascent or descent. A rung changes, of course, when a broken one is repaired (6) or a solid one is broken (9).

When all 64 hexagrams are envisioned as overlapping one another so that there is but one hexagram—the lines of which blink in ever-changing combinations of changes—this is called Journeying, in the sense of the spirit's ascent and descent along the *axis mundi*, or World Tree, uniting the upper, middle and lower realms of Creation.

By Journeying the axis of the world, spirit warriors are able to bring back knowledge and apply it to the benefit of all. This journeying side of the spirit warrior is called the *dream body* because it enters into the dream-like state of living symbols, where the not-yet-manifest *qi* swirls and gathers in shifting forms of spirit. Entering into this state of Dreaming allows spirit warriors to learn from the benevolent allies they meet and assist in the healing of those whose own dream bodies have gotten lost in the upper or lower realms.

Spirit warriors differ from others only in the sense that they consciously make a practice of defeating the *enemy-within*. *Defeating*, in this sense, however, does not imply conflict or struggle, since the *enemy-within* is comprised solely of their own self-defeating habits of thought, emotion and memory. Because habits are reinforced and strengthened every time one relives them, any active engagement with them is counterproductive to the practice of eradicating them. It is for this reason that spirit warriors extinguish their old self-defeating habits by consciously focusing on creating new habits. Stalking can be compared to the hunter who is in search of the dragon and ignores the tracks of all other game, no matter how plentiful or easy to capture. Spirit warriors take up new thoughts that evoke new feelings that open up their heart-mind to new experiences that generate new memories. In particular, they select words and phrases from the Oracle's answer and repeat such spirit-thoughts to themselves with every passing moment, allowing them to take root and take over the secret garden by taking in all the water of attention that used to go to the old habit-mind.

Change does not want to be regimented. Even the seasons, which occur in a predictable order, bear little resemblance to one another year in and year out—this year Spring comes late, last Summer it rained too much, this Autumn the hail ruined the crops, last Winter the snow never came. Waterfalls pour down but every moment of their flow is distinctly different from every other—change may appear to be ordered but upon close inspection we see the hand of chance at work, keeping the path of freedom ever open.

But human nature struggles with change, finds its randomness and accidents a source of insecurity, and attempts to marshal it into predictable and repeatable behavior. This tendency toward deadening the immediate spontaneous exploration of living potential is an externalization of the habit-mind of the *enemy-within*.

The *Ladder of Creation* is the means by which the Great Duality brings new manifestations into the six realms of existence and provides the nourishment by which they might sustain a lifetime. Symbolized by the six lines of the hexagrams, these are the six emanations of *qi* through which the Masculine Creative Force and the Feminine Creative Force pour themselves—

> 6th   Spiritual
>
> 5th   Intentional
>
> 4th   Conceptual
>
> 3rd   Individual
>
> 2nd   Relational
>
> 1st   Physical

5. THE CHANGES teaches that out of the Stillness of THE UNMANIFEST comes the Movement of THE ONE. THE CHANGES teach that out of the Unity of All Things comes the Two. THE CHANGES teach that out of the Great Duality within All Things comes the Four. THE CHANGES teach that out of the Cycle of the Seasons within All Things comes the Eight.

Commentary

It is not a rumor: when radiant awareness does not move, it reverts to the Hidden Potential—when it moves, it binds all things into the Living Unity. To experience the Hidden Potential is the destiny of every soul. To stand exposed to the numinous spirit that does not identify with anything is to return to one's own non-abiding nature. Coming to rest in the charged atmosphere of the gathering storm, after all, is the only way to feel the thunder rolling long before it breaks through into hearing: finding THE UNMANIFEST within themselves, spirit warriors revert to the Hidden Potential—the natural unfolding of creation occurs *as them* no less than the universe around them. Within and without, then, the Living Realization of the Hidden Potential unfolds as an active progression of doubling that mirrors the self-reflective nature of radiant awareness.

See FIGURE 5: THE EMANATIONS OF CREATION, Book II, Part I, Chapter II, Section 4.

6. Out of the Channels of generative energy come the paths of Fate and Freedom. The intersections of the path of Fate and the path of Freedom trace the potential combinations of opportunity and timing.

Commentary

This section alludes to a specific way of interpreting the hexagrams that is based on identifying the upper trigram with Fate and the lower trigram with Freedom. The usefulness of this method lies in seeing the upper and lower trigrams as archetypes of *qi*, the generative energy that creates and sustains all things — in its external manifestations, it appears as Temporal Circumstances and in its internal manifestations, it appears as Free Will. Temporal Circumstances, in this regard, are thought of as the uncontrollable events around one, while Free Will is considered the ability to respond to circumstances. For this reason, the upper trigram is viewed as the Opportunity provided by one's Circumstances, while the lower is seen as the Timing of responses in accord with one's Free Will. The combination of the eight archetypes of Temporal Circumstances and eight archetypes of Free Will generate the 64 Situations.

By way of example, when this method is used to interpret Hexagram #1 PROVOKING CHANGE, we see in the Temporal Circumstances of LIGHTNING a time of crisis, an unexpected Opportunity falling in a time of general upset and confusion. The response of Free Will to these events is likewise one of LIGHTNING, in the form of a precisely-targeted surprise or even shock that is timed to tip the scales into a new and more dynamic balance.

Hexagram Name: Upper / Lower Trigrams   Hexagram Name: Upper / Lower Trigrams

#1 Provoking Change: Lightning / Lightning	#33 Accepting Instruction: Lightning / Fire
#2 Sensing Creation: Lake / Lake	#34 Evoking Opposite: Sun / Lightning
#3 Recognizing Ancestry: Wind / Sun	#35 Holding Back: Mountain / Lake
#4 Mirroring Wisdom: Fire / Wind	#36 Stabilizing Communion: Lake / Mountain
#5 Restoring Wholeness: Wind / Lightning	#37 Penetrating Confusion: Water / Mountain
#6 Fostering Self-Sacrifice: Lightning / Wind	#38 Dissolving Artifice: Mountain / Moon
#7 Compelling Motive: Lake / Wind	#39 Reviving Tradition: Wind / Fire
#8 Harmonizing Duality: Wind / Lake	#40 Adapting Experience: Sun / Wind
#9 Uprooting Fear: Water / Lightning	#41 Feigning Compliance: Fire / Moon
#10 Unifying Inspiration: Lightning / Moon	#42 Interpreting Insight: Water / Sun
#11 Attracting Allies: Lake / Lightning	#43 Going Beyond: Moon / Lightning
#12 Seeing Ahead: Lightning / Lake	#44 Refining Instinct: Lightning / Water
#13 Concentrating Attention: Lightning / Mountain	#45 Casting Off: Moon / Lake
#14 Unlocking Evolution: Mountain / Lightning	#46 Honoring Contentment: Lake / Water
#15 Belonging Together: Lake / Fire	#47 Making Individual: Moon / Wind
#16 Renewing Devotion: Sun / Lake	#48 Moving Source: Wind / Water
#17 Guiding Force: Moon / Sun	#49 Staying Open: Moon / Mountain
#18 Resolving Paradox: Fire / Water	#50 Narrowing Aim: Mountain / Water
#19 Celebrating Passage: Lake / Moon	#51 Living Essence: Sun / Sun
#20 Entering Service: Water / Lake	#52 Growing Certainty: Fire / Fire
#21 Cultivating Character: Mountain / Sun	#53 Mastering Reason: Water / Fire
#22 Sharing Memory: Fire / Mountain	#54 Repeating Test: Sun / Moon
#23 Wielding Passion: Fire / Lake	#55 Internalizing Purity: Sun / Mountain
#24 Revealing Knowledge: Lake / Sun	#56 Recapturing Vision: Mountain / Fire
#25 Radiating Intent: Lightning / Sun	#57 Defying Uncertainty: Water / Water
#26 Dignifying Ambition: Fire / Lightning	#58 Dawning Existence: Moon / Moon
#27 Trusting Intuition: Fire / Sun	#59 Developing Potential: Water / Wind
#28 Synchronizing Movement: Moon / Wind	#60 Changing Alliances: Wind / Moon
#29 Sustaining Resilience: Wind / Wind	#61 Strengthening Integrity: Water / Moon
#30 Transforming Extinction: Mountain / Mountain	#62 Conceiving Spirit: Sun / Fire
#31 Embracing Noninterference: Moon / Fire	#63 Awakening Self-Sufficiency: Wind / Mountain
#32 Controlling Confrontation: Sun / Water	#64 Safeguarding Life: Mountain / Wind

FIGURE 19: SEQUENCE OF HEXAGRAMS WITH UPPER AND LOWER TRIGRAMS

The intrinsic meanings of the hexagrams can be deciphered using this method of interpretation, which is the basis of the Personality Types interpretation (see Appendix n/a).

For a complete list of trigram attributes, see: Book I, Chapter 3, Section 11.

7. Although the movement from THE ONE to the Two to the Four to the Eight to the Sixty-Four reveals the ordering principle of the world, it is the reverse movement that spirit warriors follow back to THE ONE that brings their lives meaning and good fortune. Ever returning to the Act of Creation like a thirsty soul returning to a sweet wellspring, the spirit warrior receives the nurturance and inspiration to produce works of benefit to all. Attuned to the vast field of intentions, spirit warriors follow the Oracle's thoughts in order to form alliances that produce works for the common good which provoke no negative backlash.

Commentary

The return to THE ONE is called the *resultant method*. The word *resultant* here signifies the *result or consequence of actions*; it comes from the Latin meaning *springing back*. Spirit warriors make use of the *resultant method* in order to reverse the outflow of *qi* and attune themselves to the single intent of THE ONE. Doing so brings them closer to the source of pure creative intent infusing each with its original meaning. As they respond to each according to its original meaning, spirit warriors form spontaneous subliminal alliances that grow in scope and momentum—aligning themselves with the pure creative intent of THE ONE allows spirit warriors to act without creating any resistance to good fortune in either their immediate or furthermost surroundings.

The *resultant method* is an ancient technique whereby practitioners identify with the end result of their actions. This entails concentrating on the end of the journey, as if one has already arrived, a practice no different than, for example, envisioning oneself already home. Because THE ONE is the source of all things, it is our original home as well as destination—for this reason, full realization is called *self-remembering*, for we have already been where we are going and we already are what we are becoming. The life of a spirit warrior is experienced as an individual stream flowing toward the ocean, which is, of course, both the source and destination of all lifestreams.

Because it is a non-dual world, the mind of spirit warriors is no different—they experience their minds as streams flowing toward the ocean, which is, of course, both the source and destination of all mindstreams. Trusting that the memory of their home is safeguarded within their own immortal nature, spirit warriors construct the thoughtform of their mindstream already pouring back into THE OCEANIC ONE and dispersing throughout it. From this vantage point, the mindstream is experienced as still flowing behind one, providing impetus for one's complete dispersal throughout *the original homeland*. Returning to THE ONE, spirit warriors enter the ancestral memory of the primordial ACT OF CREATION, wherein everything has its beginning as a thoughtform and every manifestation is the embodiment of its thoughtform. The *resultant method* is just this return to the ACT OF CREATION, remembering one's own original thoughtform—an act that is the result of constructing a thoughtform of one's metamorphic self. This is called *reversing the arrow of time* because the end result actually precedes the step-by-step cultivation that would otherwise cause complete self-realization: From such a perspective spirit warriors experience their awareness at one with THE OCEANIC ONE, working their way back along their lifestream as if their mindstream were flowing backward from the sea.

> 8. *SPIRIT informs everything with the sacred: Spirit warriors recognize that they are part of everything and so understand that they, too, are sacred. SPIRIT and NATURE are undergoing a mysterious metamorphosis: Spirit warriors recognize that the life of a butterfly in no way resembles the life of a caterpillar and so understand that all of creation is yet coiled within its chrysalis, gathering strength for its emergence.*

> *The sky reveals the vastness of creation: Spirit warriors recognize the scope and grandeur of creation and so understand the nobility of being part of existence. The land reveals the circulation of generative energy: Spirit warriors recognize the same pattern of change within themselves and so understand that they, too, are circulating among all things.*

Commentary

The Way of Transformation is the Way of Communion. The dispersal of awareness throughout THE OCEANIC ONE is reflected in our complete identification with all manifestations. Universal Communion, then, is a *being with* and a *belonging with* all things, an immediate and spontaneous exchange of *The Intimate* that forms the core of each manifestation's original nature.

Breaking through the static sense of separation from the Whole, experienced as the duality of self-and-other, our personality undergoes a profound transformation of *belonging with* the world and all its manifestations. This is called *ending inference*, because it destroys the illusion of separation that results from erroneous conclusions the personality has drawn from experience. *Ending inference* means that we accept raw perception of things-as-they-are, rather than deciding what they are—and what they mean—by the inferences handed down through familial and cultural conditioning. Accepting raw perception of things-as-they-are means moving away from historicizing all that we encounter: Rather than constructing a past-to-present-to-future history of cause-and-effect relationships for things, we identify with them in the present moment, experiencing them as ever-new as ourselves. In this way, pure awareness circulates among all things in the ever-new present moment of the ongoing Act of Creation, having stopped historicizing itself and thereby reverted to its own being-as-it-is.

9. THE CHANGES teach that the Way of Freedom is open and easy to travel, whereas the Way of Fate is closed and difficult to traverse. Its symbols point to the good fortune found in the untroubled spirit and the misfortune found in the troubled spirit. Its words point to the self that precedes words in order to attune the troubled spirit to the naturalness of the Way of Freedom. The Oracle speaks in order to accompany spirit warriors on their journey through their lifetimes.

Commentary

To allow ourselves to be dragged along by circumstances and convention is to close ourselves off from the unimaginable potential before us, bringing unnecessary hardship and grief into our lives. THE CHANGES points to the incipient nature of events, actions and intentions, calling into question those that are self-defeating and reinforcing those that promise good fortune. It encourages those who identify with the mortal self of a single lifetime to step back inside themselves and remember the part of themselves that has always been, the part of themselves that is always part of everything. Coming into contact with one's immortal nature releases the personality from the bonds of fear, greed and self-interest, allowing it to transform into the *dream body* that is one with the symbols of the archetypal thoughtforms. THE CHANGES is itself an instrument of change—it changes those who ally themselves with it, reawakening the older act of Being that precedes the act of Thinking and its attendant language. The primordial act of Being, however, has a language of its own—a *Speaking Mystery* whose creative play is the self-revelation of every piece within its *Sacred Game.*

Chapter XII. *Recapitulation*

1. Does good fortune really favor those who seek to benefit the whole? One of the ancients' great teachings is that acting out of self-interest to the detriment of the whole injures all. Because profit brings gain for one at the expense of many and benefit brings gain for many at the expense of one, the logic of benefit is superior to the logic of profit. Because self-interest cannot injure the whole without injuring oneself and self-sacrifice cannot benefit the whole without benefiting oneself, the logic of self-sacrifice is superior to the logic of self-interest. Therefore, yes, good fortune does really favor those who seek to benefit the whole.

Commentary

Here, the ethics of inspired action and its resultant good fortune are laid bare in the logic of spiritual cause-and-effect. Setting one's intention to enter each moment already-inclined to benefit all is, paradoxically, the very act which, when sustained over time, brings personal good fortune.

2. Are the intentions of the ancients fully expressed in words? Words are like a finger pointing at the moon—depending on words, one misses the light breaking up the darkness. Words are the springboard by which the intuitive catapult into understanding—their meaning all comes originally from the symbols themselves. Words allude, they do not explain—the stomach is not filled by talk of a meal nor is the soul satiated by anything but first-hand knowledge. Therefore, no, the intentions of the ancients are not fully expressed in words.

Commentary

It is not possible to know everything but it is possible to understand everything. This is because everything interacts according to archetypal relationships and although specific knowledge grows and changes over time, the archetypal relationships governing their interactions does not ever change. It is to this understanding that the sages have always pointed, using words as the doorknocker to the inner door.

Essence recognizes essence and *qi* recognizes *qi*. THE CHANGES teaches that everything falls into archetypal categories of *qi*, represented by the trigrams. As we attune ourselves to the *meaning-tone* of each of the trigrams, we increasingly sensitize ourselves to the selfsameness of essence within all things and ourselves.

This allows us to grasp the essential, archetypal nature of each thing and how it fits within the categories of *qi*. Identifying things with their respective trigrams in this way, we can trace their archetypal relationships through the combination of inner and outer trigrams within the 64 hexagrams. It is for this reason that it is said that *The trigrams are our real senses*.

3. The Creating and Sustaining Forces are the basis of all change and continuity. Without their exchange of generative energy, nothing would exist. Likewise, without the mirror of the universe in which to perfect their intent, even the Creative and Sustaining Forces would fall back into the sleep of unrealized potential.

Commentary

We enter this world of manifestation and everything we need to survive is already provided. The miracle of air and water and food is impossible to comprehend. Any attitude other than gratitude is beneath us, any emotion but reverence is a betrayal of our original nature. The non-dual nature of reality requires that we love this creation within which we find ourselves and hold its manifestations sacred.

4. THE CHANGES teach that that which has Form adores the Formless, just as that which is Formless adores Form. NATURE, therefore, adores SPIRIT, just as SPIRIT adores NATURE—as the body adores the soul and the soul adores the body. For this reason, spirit warriors focus less on adoring the soul, SPIRIT, and the Formless—rather, they concentrate more on adoring the body, NATURE, and that which has Form, in order to better identify with the Formless. This is called repairing a lower rung in order to reach a higher one.

Commentary

When people are young, they conceive of themselves as Form and they adore Form, which is all they can conceive. As they mature, however, they can conceive of the Formless, which is what they come to adore. With fuller maturity, though, they conceive of themselves as Formless and come to adore the Form of all manifestation. This matter of adoration between Form and Formless is the lived experience of the Love that binds the Creative Forces in their eternal Union. In this sense, Form does not adore Form—it adores the Formless. Nor does the Formless adore the Formless—it adores Form. This is why spirit warriors steep themselves in nature mysticism and the sacredness of matter—adoring Form, they crystalize their identification with the Formless. By identifying with the Formless, spirit warriors are loved by Form.

5. There is an underlying harmony to the world. It is expressed by the seasons of the generative energy, which flows through its patterns into the phenomena of the world. It is of this underlying harmony that the Oracle speaks in the INTENT of each hexagram.

There is an underlying purpose to the world. It is expressed in the compass points of the generative energy, which circulates like magnetism among everything, attracting to itself the essence of each. It is of this underlying purpose that the Oracle speaks in the ACTION of each hexagram.

Commentary

This section of the Recapitulation is a straightforward repetition of sections 1 and 2 of Chapter 8, above, which emphasizes the importance of the INTENT and ACTION texts.

6. There is an underlying unity to the world. It is expressed in the symbols of the generative energy, which unites the dreaming heart-mind with the waking heart-mind. It is of this underlying unity that the Oracle speaks in the INTERPRETATION of each hexagram.

Commentary

This section of the Recapitulation is a straightforward repetition of section 3 of Chapter 8, above, which emphasizes the importance of the INTERPRETATION text.

7. The way the present Situation moves into the next is revealed in the LINE CHANGES. Facilitating change, whether internally or externally, requires a consistent set of ethical intentions that can respond and adapt to changing circumstances without provoking negative backlashes. Spirit warriors, therefore, still their heart-mind in order to hear the Oracle: Sincerity is simply the natural desire to explore THE UNKNOWN.

Commentary

This section of the Recapitulation reiterates the functional importance of the line changes: They are the transitions, the bridges, between the present hexagram and the future hexagram. It is for this reason that the text accompanying the line changes stand as warnings or encouragements—the lessons of the line changes teach the principle of beneficial intention that give rise to inspired action and good fortune.

PART II

Chapter I. *On the Signs and Numbers, On Changing and Responding*

1. From 0 to 7, the eight trigrams are arranged by their numerical value: thus their meanings are determined by their place in the order of realization. From 0 to 63, the sixty-four hexagrams are arranged by their numerical value: their meanings are determined by the interaction of their trigrams.

<u>Commentary</u>

The *order of realization* is the natural progression of *qi* as it moves from the inception to the completion of thoughtforms (See Book I, Chapter II).

Sun	Lake	Fire	Lightning	Wind	Water	Mountain	Moon
0	1	2	3	4	5	6	7

Because all things are manifestations of thoughtforms, this progression is an archetypal unfolding of essence as it moves toward existence—regardless of whether one is considering a work of art, a relationship, a business endeavor, or a nation. *Sun* is the power of creative vision, the initial glimpse of potential, the seed of a beginning. *Lake* is the enthusiasm that accompanies a new beginning, the joy and wonder of novelty. *Fire* is the understanding and knowledge needed to undertake the work, which might mean getting to know others better or researching the matter carefully. *Lightning* is the surprising development that seems to come out of nowhere, the unexpected revelation of unforeseen connections. *Wind* is the dedicated persistence required to carry through, to integrate ongoing developments with the initial vision. *Water* is the uncertainty that comes along with committing to the end, the willingness to take risks, the insecurity of possible failure. *Mountain* is the interruption in the process needed to allow things to gel or the frustration of being blocked approaching the ending. *Moon* is the completing energy that brings the seed to full fruition, the finishing of things that completes and fulfills their original potential.

Obviously, most thoughtforms do not reach full realization, falling prey to the negative, self-defeating aspects of each archetype: Many do not survive the fantasizing impulse of *Sun* or the distractible excitement of *Lake* or the unquestioned preconceptions of *Fire* or the unforeseen turning point of *Lightning* or the misdirected stubbornness of *Wind* or the unnerving indecision of *Water* or the frenetic impatience of *Mountain* or the apathetic procrastination of *Moon*. The *order of realization*, then, can be disrupted at any point in the progression—the closer to the end point, in fact, the greater the likelihood it will not be reached successfully.

Ending things is a lost art. Finishing things is a neglected science. Cultivating, polishing and perfecting things is a forgotten magic. The *order of realization* evokes the predictable phases of every thoughtform struggling to blossom into the fullness of miracle-and-shadow.

Sun is paradoxically receptive, reflecting the mirror of the universe in every blink of its golden eye: it does not create out of nothing but is the womb through which THE UNMANIFEST turns itself inside-out.

Lake is paradoxically still, every wave named and becalmed in the twilight of *The Beloveds'* union: it is not passionless excitement but is the mystical face of awe in the face of proximity to the momentary ACT OF CREATION.

Fire is paradoxically dark, dependent on so many factors beyond itself for its burning, a thief robbing the gods' treasure house of mortality for another glimpse of blinding life: it is not illumination itself but is illuminative, the force moving from wrong conclusions to preconceptions to learning to knowing to understanding to accidental wisdom.

Lightning is paradoxically reassuring, a grandmotherly reminder of the childlike power and energy connecting the celestial and earthly: it is not merely the unexpected move but is a sudden breakthrough in the rules of play, a broken window, a shattered door, the instantaneous reversal of amnesia.

Wind is paradoxically distant, the harbinger of change, the carrier of the yet-to-arrive, the mercurial omen of the mercurial: it is not the messenger but is the message itself, a boon just below the horizon of the present, a baying of utter longing in the night.

Water is paradoxically death-revealing, a falling downward and inward toward the depths of the underworld of dream: it is not veiling the immortality of all things but is making transparent the creative annihilation of all alternatives to the road taken.

Mountain is paradoxically ecstatic, the pinnacle of selflessness standing outside itself, the emptiness of *mental fasting*: it is not apart but is THE ALONE, the open heart-mind making a nest for the phoenix of light to tie end back to beginning.

Moon is paradoxically vocal, commanding obedience from the unfathomed sea, calling all home in the secret song of the conch: it does not merely echo the solar wind but is THE ROOM WITHOUT WALLS reverberating with the celestial choir of all the light-bearers of The Void.

From the perspective of the creative intent, no bounds confine the archetypal symbols of the trigrams—each is a springboard into The Beyond, a *thrown-into* the struggle of thoughtforms battling the current back to their spawning ground. From the mirror perspective of the order itself, the crystalization into full realization is marked by the evolving marriage of imagination and intent accompanying the thoughtform.

From 0 to 7, the trigrams are ordered according to their qualitative allotment of *qi*, which determines their respective meanings. This same *order of realization* plays itself out in the numerical values, 0 to 63, of the sixty-four hexagrams.

As Figure 20, below, demonstrates, the upper trigrams in each row follow the *order of realization*. For instance, in the second row, numbered 8-15, the upper trigrams are, left-to-right: *Sun, Lake, Fire, Lightning, Wind, Water, Mountain, Moon*. Every row exhibits the identical order of upper trigrams.

Likewise, the lower trigrams in every column follow the *order of realization*. For instance, in the second column, numbered 1-9-17-25-33-41-49-57, the upper trigrams are, from top to bottom: *Sun, Lake, Fire, Lightning, Wind, Water, Mountain, Moon*. Every column exhibits the identical order of lower trigrams.

This section indicates that the meaning of each of the 64 hexagrams is shaped by the interaction between the upper and lower trigrams, the meanings of which are determined by their place in the *order of realization*.

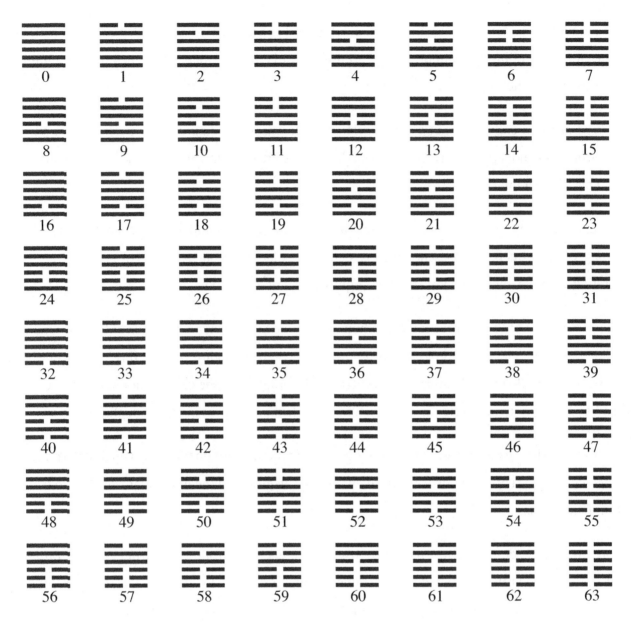

FIGURE 20: THE BINARY NUMBERS OF THE HEXAGRAMS

The sequence of hexagrams in Figure 20, above, displays the binary value of each hexagram. This is the same order attributed to the ancient sage, Fu Xi, and made public by the great philosopher, Shao Yung. For the hexagram numbers of *The Toltec I Ching* sequence, See FIGURE 18: THE FU XI ARRANGEMENT OF THE HEXAGRAMS, BOOK II, PART I, CHAPTER 5, SECTION 8. As indicated there, these binary numbers are the hexagrams' *QI NUMBERS*, which represent the *identities* of the hexagrams. Their identities are, as stated above, the product of combining the meanings of the upper and lower trigrams, the interactions of which result in synergistic meanings that are more than the simple sum of the trigrams.

For example, Hexagram #1 PROVOKING CHANGE is composed of the upper trigram *Lightning* and the lower trigram *Lightning*. Its *QI NUMBER*, or binary number, is 27 and can be found at the intersection of the fourth row and the fourth column in Figure 20, above. The upper trigram *Lightning* signifies a time of crisis in the external realm, whereas the inner trigram *Lightning* signifies a response that is unexpected and surprising. The synergistic meaning of the interaction of the two trigrams, then, points to the need to upset matters, tip them out of balance in an unforeseen way, so that a stagnant equilibrium can be provoked into changing into a new and more dynamic equilibrium.

> *2. Broken and solid lines take turns passing through the six stages, tracing the trends of hexagrams changing from one into the next.*

Commentary

The essence of all change can be analyzed, interpreted and foretold by understanding the nature of the fourfold progression of the broken and solid lines. (See FIGURE 8: THE INNER COMPASS, BOOK II, PART I, CHAPTER II, SECTION 4).

Because this progression mirrors that of the natural cycle of change in the seasons of the year, it permits a view of the process of transformation that includes the presaging of future situations that are yet in their incipient phase of development. This is the function of the line changes (6 and 9), which identify the *focal points of change* as specific stages within the situation that are undergoing stress and in the process of reversing their direction. No less importantly, however, are the unchanging lines (7 and 8), which identify the stable forces within the situation that reinforce the status quo.

> *3. Trends follow patterns and so can be anticipated—opportunities to do good or ill present themselves constantly. Impeccability means grounding each decision in the ethics of benefiting the whole—in this way, avoidable misfortune and suffering can be circumvented.*

Commentary

The trend of change can be analyzed and interpreted when viewed from the distance of a system perspective. What evokes good fortune and misfortune can be seen to issue from actions that reflect consistent intents, or ethics: those whose intent is in accord with the intent of *universal benefit* of THE ONE enjoy good fortune, while those whose intent is one-sided suffer misfortune.

Impeccable intent is sometimes called the pickpocket's intent: just as pickpockets never lose focus or concentration on the pockets and purses around them, no matter where they are or what time of day it might be, spirit warriors never lose focus or concentration on the forces-at-hand that might be *turned to benefit the whole*, no matter where they are or what time of day it might be.

4. Change occurs spontaneously in Situations where equilibrium has stagnated or turned against itself. Change intends no specific outcome ahead of time because the resulting disequilibrium naturally rights itself in a new, better adapted, equilibrium.

Commentary

Change is open-ended. It is natural and spontaneous, although its timing can be difficult to see accurately because the combination of forces driving change and forces preserving the status quo are not always transparent. Change moves between two poles (7 and 8), where it stabilizes and consolidates, eventually becoming either stagnant or self-defeating. It is at this point that change sets in (6 or 9) as a natural and spontaneous release of pent-up energies. During periods of stability (7 and 8), it is more difficult to influence decisions already set in motion. During periods of change (6 and 9), it is easier to influence the direction and momentum of decisions determining the new, emerging equilibrium.

5. The law of spiritual cause-and-effect holds that intentions are inner actions that attract or repel other intentions within a shared field of action, called the INTENTIONAL FIELD. *While change appears to come from outer actions, it is clear that outer actions come from inner actions. Because spirit warriors aim for collaborative endeavors that benefit the whole, their intent does not cause negative backlashes. The path of misfortune, however, is strewn with the dashed hopes and dreams of those whose intent was based on self-interest: even if they achieve their short-term goals, the effects are negative on those around them and the backlashes they produce erase their achievements like a wave washing away footprints in the sand.*

Working to benefit the whole forms the basis of the ethics of the Universal Civilizing Spirit. Those who align their intent with it enjoy profound good fortune, while those who oppose it suffer avoidable misfortune.

Commentary

This section is a further elucidation of Section 3, above, providing the logic of the metaphysics of the causality of good fortune and misfortune. Contrary to most people's notions, intent is not just "inconsequential thoughts". Intentional acts are fully as powerful and consequential as any outer action. They are the actions of the *intentional body*, which is also called the *dream body*. They are performed within the shared space of the inner landscape of the *intentional field*, which is also called the *World Soul*.

In the same way that people stopped seeing Earth as the *center* of the universe and began seeing it as *one part* of the universe, spirit warriors stop seeing their personal identities as the center of experience and begin seeing it as one part of the greater Whole. This movement from the *I Am* to the *We Are I Am* de-centers the sense of self that has maintained a privileged position among all other selves, returning it to its rightful place as a peer among an eternity of peers: Situated in this wider realm of *universal communion*, awareness renews its identification with the whole of *Being* that precedes both the five senses and the reason derived from them.

This awareness does not have a body—it *is* a body. It constellates *understanding and memory* into a coherent *experience* of the Whole. It self-organizes, moves, and interacts by the nature and quality of its intent. Within the shared dream-space of the *World Soul*, there is no dichotomy of inner-outer, spirit-matter, subject-object or even reality-appearance: awareness is self-aware *as awareness-itself* and it cycles between communing with other *intentional bodies* and communing with the *World Soul* itself. Like a glass of water poured into the sea, the *intentional body* touches and is touched—its edges are self-defined and as permeable or impermeable as intent allows. Contact with other *intentional bodies*—or with the *World Soul* itself— results in an exchange of *understanding and memory* to the degree of openness of intent.

This is not *the world-between* but *the world-before*. It is the world of *universal communion*, wherein THE ONE and THE MANY are in perpetual—at least, potentially—contact. Individuals can encapsulate themselves within walls of distrustful and fearful intent, slowing down the process of their self-remembering, but eventually the loving-kindness and ecstatic lushness of the *world-behind-the-world* draws them out into the light of shared intent. Subsensorial, preconceptual, co-conscious: here is the world of underlying causes, the effects of which manifest as the world of the five senses.

The substance of the *intentional field* is primordial, undifferentiated *qi*, the *generative energy* or *dream matter*, that creates and sustains all. As the *World Soul*, it is first and foremost the overflowing of a *wellspring of presence*, called by the ancients *a sphere of light whose center is everywhere and circumference nowhere*. Because light is the mediating element making vision possible, it is the center of seeing that is everywhere—similarly, because awareness is the mediating presence making experience possible, it is the center of *Being* that is everywhere. In this sense, awareness abides in this place that is everywhere, this place that is nowhere, this place that casts its shadow of awareness into the secondary world of subjectivity and objectivity. Despite its branches reaching into the realms of fascination with inner and outer narratives, in other words, awareness always has its roots in the *first world* of the soul.

Awareness *is*, intent *does*. The heart-mind of the *World Soul* is universally benevolent, so spirit warriors adopt the same intent in order to accord with it. To manifest change in the world of the senses, they focus their intent on its outcome as already fitting into the *field of intentions* in a way that benefits all and harms none. Such precisely-aimed intent garners reinforcement from surrounding intents, coalesces *qi* into purposeful thoughtforms, and triggers their emergence from the subsensorial into manifestation. Without the collaborative spirit of other intents, our own intent meets with resistance from surrounding intents— without an intent toward benefiting all, our intent does not garner the support of surrounding intents.

What does it mean to benefit all? Essentially, it means the concentrated, whole-hearted and sincere intent that all manifestations enjoy peace and prospering. This is called *impeccable intent* and forms the basis of the ethics of inspired action that spirit warriors embody.

This is not a naive ethics, however. So long as there remain people of ill-will, mean-spiritedness, greed, and aggression, the ideal of peace and prospering for all remains a dream. Even acting on this ideal too publicly can provoke a backlash from such people, so spirit warriors pursue a strategy of ethical victory: By focusing their intent on *change within the intentional field*, spirit warriors garner the support of surrounding intents, which self-organizes in apt but unpredictable ways that bring about the best changes for all as they emerge into manifestation. By working within the *intentional field* through their *impeccable intent*, spirit warriors are able to work with their *allies-at-a-distance* to bring about beneficial change for all without incurring the backlashes of antagonism, conflict and retribution that bring harm to all. Such an ethics forms the basis of the strategy of inspired action.

The millennia-old alchemical work of *allies-at-a-distance* is called the *Universal Civilizing Spirit*. It is the collaboration of spirit warriors extending back through the Ages by which the intent of the *World Soul* might be fulfilled in human nature. This work consists of turning the tide of greedy, distrustful, fearful, and aggressive intents by building a coalition of supporting intents aligned with that of the *World Soul*.

We have reached the halfway mark now and the momentum of transmuted intents is accelerating, in accord with the Oracle's first auguries. The closer we approach unanimity of intent, it is likewise foretold, the more self-destructive the entrenched intents of humanity's *enemy-within* will become. Only by the greatest number exerting their intents for *universal benefit* will our collective *enemy-within* awaken to the Open Secret of the universal metamorphosis that ensures humanity's perfect harmony with itself, nature, and spirit.

6. The MASCULINE CREATIVE FORCE expresses itself through direct purposeful action that is straightforward and forceful. The FEMININE CREATIVE FORCE expresses itself through indirect contingencies that follow the line of least resistance and nurture everything it touches.

Commentary

The MASCULINE CREATIVE FORCE is the cosmological counterpart to the *masculine half* of human nature, just as the FEMININE CREATIVE FORCE is the cosmological counterpart to the *feminine half* of human nature. The union of the Great Duality of the Creative Forces is the primordial Act of Creation that gives rise to the whole of *generative energy* in the world of worlds. The MASCULINE CREATIVE FORCE has long been called Yang, the half of experience governed by Action. The FEMININE CREATIVE FORCE has long been called Yin, the half of experience governed by Relation. Whereas the MASCULINE CREATIVE FORCE tests and trains human nature in order to increase its versatility and fortitude, the FEMININE CREATIVE FORCE conceives in order to nurture and sustain all that is valuable in human nature. For those who find the Great Duality of the Creative Forces within themselves, the entire universe is ablaze with the ecstasy of their Creative Union.

7. The LINES show how the MASCULINE AND FEMININE CREATIVE FORCES are interacting in the six stages of the HEXAGRAM. The TRIGRAMS show how the archetypes of internal and external generative energy are interacting in the sequence of HEXAGRAMS.

Commentary

The six stages of the hexagram stand for specific types of issues considered developmental or naturalistic, in the sense of representing similar stages of personal and social development. Below is a rendering of the six places signifying the stages of life, the personal issues they raise, and their correlative social roles—

	Life Stage	Personal Issues	Social Roles
6th	Elder	Disengagement, Interdependence	Mediators
5th	Middle Age	Empowerment, Authority	Powerful
4th	Adult	Responsibility, Independence	Bureaucracy
3rd	Adolescent	Separation, Alienation	Dissidents
2nd	Child	Trust, Attachment, Bonding	Social Service
1st	Infant	Vulnerability, Dependence	Masses

Because each of these six places can be occupied by either a solid (yang) line or a broken (yin) line, the changing relationships between the MASCULINE CREATIVE FORCE and the FEMININE CREATIVE FORCE can be analyzed and interpreted.

This is made apparent in FIGURE 12: MARKING SHIFTS OF ATTENTION (See Book II, Part I, Chapter III, Section 3) reproduced below—

6 = waking up	emerging	*will be* an issue	coming into foreground
7 = active	conscious	*is* an issue	in foreground
8 = subliminal	unconscious	is *not* an issue	in background
9 = going to sleep	submerging	*won't be* an issue	fading into background

Here we see that the unchanging lines represent relatively stable periods in which an issue is remaining in the foreground (7) or background (8) of attention as the situation develops. The changing lines (6 and 9), however, represent turning points, or transitions, where issues that have been in the background of attention are moving to the foreground (6) or issues that have been in the foreground of attention are moving into the background (9).

It is, of course, these changing lines that define the direction of the trending developments of the situation and act as the actual bridges to the next situation.

```
        #22                    #17
      ——⊖——                  ——  ——
      ——  ——                  ——  ——
      ——⊖——                  ——  ——
      ——x——                  ————————
      ——x——                  ————————
```

In the example above, Hexagram #22 SHARING MEMORY represents the present situation that is developing into the future situation, Hexagram #17 GUIDING FORCE. The MASCULINE and FEMININE CREATIVE FORCES interact in this case by holding in attention the sense of Separation and Alienation (the 7 in the 3ʳᵈ place) and continuing to ignore the issue of Authority (the 8 in the 5ᵗʰ place). The other four lines mark the turning points where Disengagement and Responsibility shift from requiring attention to needing none (the 9 in the 4ᵗʰ and 6ᵗʰ places) and where Trust and Dependence shift from the background of attention to the foreground (the 6 in the 1ˢᵗ and 4ᵗʰ places).

This section further reinforces the importance of the interaction of the upper and lower trigrams in the deeper interpretation of the hexagrams. Because the upper trigram depicts the outer circumstances of the hexagram and the lower trigram depicts the inner nature of the hexagram, their interaction produces a synergistic meaning that both amplifies the intent of the hexagram and the sequence of the hexagrams as a whole. In the latter sense, each hexagram receives the forward momentum of the sequence from the hexagram before it, fixes it in place for the time being, and then passes it on to the succeeding hexagram (See FIGURE 16: THE SEQUENCE OF HEXAGRAMS, Book II, Chapter IV, Section 4).

In the former sense, each hexagram can be analyzed as the conjunction and interaction of the archetypal meanings of its upper and lower trigrams —

SUN:	Lower: ENVISIONING	Upper: POTENTIAL
LAKE:	Lower: COMMUNING	Upper: COLLABORATION
FIRE:	Lower: ANSWERING	Upper: INTEGRATION
LIGHTNING:	Lower: SURPRISING	Upper: CRISIS
WIND:	Lower: PACIFYING	Upper: RECOVERY
WATER:	Lower: QUESTIONING	Upper: EXPERIMENT
MOUNTAIN:	Lower: WAITING	Upper: INCUBATION
MOON:	Lower: PERFECTING	Upper: REALIZATION

The trigrams, in other words, can have slightly different nuances, depending on whether they are the *upper* or *lower* trigram. This is because the upper, or outer, trigram represents the external circumstances or, alternatively, the one's outer nature as a relationship to external circumstances—and, likewise, the lower, or inner, trigram represents the internal state or, alternatively, one's response to external circumstances.

Returning to the example above, Hexagram #22 SHARING MEMORY is the conjunction of Fire over Mountain. The outer nature of the hexagram is INTEGRATION while its inner nature is WAITING. The interaction of these trigrams is such that WAITING implies a *stopping and seeing*, a stillpoint for contemplating the inner landscape of images, symbols and memories, while INTEGRATION points to the act of fitting that *seeing* into the wider *seeing*, of fitting one's own memories into the wider *Memory*. Likewise, Hexagram #17 GUIDING FORCE, as the future situation from the example above, is made up of Moon over Sun. The outer nature of the hexagram, therefore, is REALIZATION, while its inner nature is ENVISIONING. The interaction of these two archetypes is such that REALIZATION connotes the completion of a cycle in the outer circumstances, while ENVISIONING points to the inception of something new, a creative act within that is reinforced and supported by a sense of fulfillment and contentment without—this is a highly favorable situation reflecting the principle of *Orientation*, whereby a new beginning follows close on the heels of bringing things to a constructive conclusion.

See also FIGURE 3: SUMMARY OF TRIGRAM ATTRIBUTES, Book I, Chapter III, Section 11.

> *8. The PRIMORDIAL HEXAGRAM is made up of six empty places: No LINES yet exist therein, no TRIGRAMS yet interact therein. In this sense, there is only one hexagram, not sixty-four, and all transformations occur therein. The lessons encrypted in THE CHANGES keep alive the spiritual ancestors' dreams for a Golden Age of Humanity.*

Commentary

This section refers to the diviner's communion with the Oracle: With familiarity, the diviner internalizes THE CHANGES, experiencing the one hexagram that includes all 64 hexagrams at once. This is a vision of the Oracle's dream-body that occurs spontaneously and of its own accord. It appears before one as a hexagram of light, the six lines of which are constantly alternating between broken and solid in all their possible combination of permutations.

This kind of intimacy with the Oracle brings one into communion with the ancient lineage of wise women and wise men, those *upside-down ones*, who do not dedicate their birth and death to their own self-aggrandizement but, rather, to fully realizing the vision of a world in which an uninterrupted reign of peace and prospering for all is firmly established in the heart-mind of every human being. Such are the lessons imparted by THE CHANGES, for every symbol and word reflects the inspired action of the inevitable Golden Age of Humanity, which can only be governed by the ethics of self-sacrifice and absolute nonviolence.

9. The union the higher soul and the body produces the lower soul. Without the proper relationship, the lower soul wanders lost and confused after the death of the body. It is the great treasure of spirit warriors to accompany the higher soul back to the SPHERE OF COMMUNION upon the death of the body.

How is this relationship established? By administering the UNIVERSAL PANACEA. How is that legendary cure-all administered? By vigilantly sustaining the intent to meet every NEED with BENEFIT. Compassion is the heartfelt goodwill pouring forth from the spirit warrior's breast to cover heaven and earth, whereas wisdom is knowing what kind of BENEFIT to offer in each situation. Just as every illness is different, the medicine, too, must be individual.

Commentary

This section speaks to the esoteric teachings of immortality. It begins by clarifying the nature of the lived life—a necessary step, since the original teaching has come to be covered over by the trappings of religion and materialism. The higher soul, which is an individuated spirit-body within the *Sphere of Communion*, associates with a physical body upon its birth. This union produces a new soul, often called the lower, or earthly, soul, which consists of the sum of all the body's experiences. It is, then, an earthly spirit-body, an individuated aspect of the *World Soul*, or *Nature*. As such it is often called the personality, or personal identity, that grows and matures with the body's experiences. However, the true name of the lower soul is *Memory*, just as the true name of the higher soul is *Understanding*. At the death of the body, the lower soul needs to be firmly united with the higher soul or else it wanders in a confused state, without the *Understanding* of the higher soul to guide it, perpetually reliving its *Memory* of the body's experiences. Likewise, if the two souls are not united, the higher soul returns to the *Sphere of Communion* without the *Memory* of the lifetime just lived.

Spirit warriors defeat their enemy-within, quieting the self-defeating habit-mind whose static drowns out the voice of the higher soul. They empty out the lower soul to make a lodging-place for the higher soul, opening themselves to its *Understanding* in order to create new memories that enrich the *Memory* of this lifetime. While meditation and psychophysical exercises can help unite the two souls, they ultimately prove ineffective if they lack the quintessential intent to meet every *need* with *benefit*. Aligning themselves with the intent of *universal benevolence*, spirit warriors experience the union of the two souls as the personal embodiment of the *well of benefit* that flows into every place of *need*. There is no fixed form of *benefit*, since *need* is ever different in its own form. For this reason, the union of the two souls is also experienced as the *thousand-foot cliff of wisdom*, an imperturbable force of discernment that spontaneously responds to every *need* with the precise kind and degree of *benefit* that reflects the ethics of inspired action.

The UNIVERSAL PANACEA, therefore, is both the mechanism for attaining personal immortality as well as uniting humanity, nature, and spirit in an unbreakable web of mutual benefit.

Chapter II. *The Universal Civilizing Spirit*

1. In the heavens there is the order and harmony of movement among the stars. On earth there is the order and harmony of the seasons and the compass points. The spiritual ancestors recognized an inherent tendency within all things toward a harmonious union of order and chance: they discovered this same pattern of CONSCIOUS CHANGE within themselves and aligned their intent with it in order to ensure that humanity does not fall into the pit of self-destruction. Within their heart-minds, thereby, the inner pattern of generative energy perfectly reflected the outer pattern of generative energy and the eight TRIGRAMS were born.

Commentary

Nature embodies CONSCIOUS CHANGE in the evolution toward higher forms of intelligence. THE CHANGES embodies CONSCIOUS CHANGE in the form of the *Oracle*. The ancients came to the realization that we embody CONSCIOUS CHANGE in the form of an autonomous inner drive toward metamorphosis. It did not, however, escape their notice that this drive toward metamorphosis is set against, or parallel to, an equally strong drive toward self-destruction, which they likewise found at work in the processes of deterioration in nature. From the very beginning of human culture, then, there have been those lineages, often of blood and kinship, that have striven to institutionalize the latter drive, creating social conventions of dominance, greed, and violence that arc across the generations. In order to offset this darker side of human nature, the ancient spirit warriors formalized a shadow lineage of light, based not on kinship but on spiritual and intentional affinity, that has striven to create social conventions of noninterference, self-sacrifice, and nonviolence that likewise arc across the generations. Because they recognized the drive of CONSCIOUS CHANGE as an autonomous force acting both from within and without, they named it the *Universal Civilizing Force*, or simply *The Way*.

Among the conventions the spiritual ancestors formalized were the *eight archetypes of correspondence* between the inner and outer realms. These primordial images by which *qi* self-organizes itself in the outer, sensory and inner, psychic realms are symbolized by the eight trigrams.

2. They trained themselves to perceive what actually exists rather than what they might desire—in this way, they were able to imagine what might exist. This they took from the hexagram GROWING CERTAINTY.

Hexagram #52 GROWING CERTAINTY is composed of the trigrams Fire over Fire, suggesting a time of inner Understanding and outer Understanding. Knowing that such times engender strong beliefs among competing groups, the ancients envisioned the ideal combination of such CONSCIOUS CHANGE and learned thereby the art of seeing through illusion by envisioning the inevitable metamorphosis. From this, the vision of the *Universal Civilizing Spirit* was perceived as an enduring reign of beauty, creativity, harmony, peace and prospering.

3. They cultivated the original self that is, from beginning to end, uncut, undamaged, and intact—in this way, they were able to point their descendants to the path of the eternal return. This they took from the hexagram RESTORING WHOLENESS.

Commentary

Hexagram #5 RESTORING WHOLENESS comprises the trigrams Wind over Lightning, suggesting a time of inner Inspiration and outer Adaptation. Holding unflagging purpose within while adapting it to all outer circumstances, the ancients embodied the original vision of the RETURN TO THE ACT OF CREATION. By enlivening, or activating, the inner, true self in such a way that its influence, or intent, pours out to cover heaven and earth, the spiritual ancestors set up a model for succeeding generations to emulate.

4. They refined their hearts and minds in order to ennoble their longings—in this way, they were able to point to the self-discipline required to follow desires without suffering or causing harm. This they took from the hexagram DIGNIFYING AMBITION.

Commentary

Hexagram #26 DIGNIFYING AMBITION is composed of the trigrams Fire over Lightning, suggesting a time of Inspiration within and Understanding without. When an inner sense of purpose manifests itself in a wise and compassionate way, then the self can be trusted to wish for things that benefit all. This is the path of intending great works without creating negative backlashes.

5. They studied they cycles of beginnings and endings in order to create customs and institutions that could adapt to changing times—in this way, they were able to see people govern themselves with vision and benevolence. This they took from the hexagrams LIVING ESSENCE and DAWNING EXISTENCE.

Commentary

Hexagram #51 LIVING ESSENCE is composed of the trigrams Sun over Sun, or Creation within and Creation without, while Hexagram #58 DAWNING EXISTENCE is composed of the trigrams Moon over Moon, or Completion within and Completion without. Taking these two hexagrams as a pair, the ancients perceived the profound relation between Vision and Realization, for the corruption and failure of otherwise beneficial beginnings could not escape their eye. For this reason, they clove neither to the side of pragmatism nor the side of idealism, neither to the side of conservatism nor the side of progressivism, neither to the side of religious zealotry nor to the side of secular materialism: if people are to govern themselves with wisdom and benevolence, they reasoned, then the Creative Vision giving life to their customs and institutions must include from the very beginning an emotional image of the joyous homecoming all will experience upon reaching the Golden Age of Humanity.

In the same way that time passes for the body but not for the soul, time passes for Nature but not for the World Soul: people will govern themselves with vision and benevolence when they see the eternal within their reach. Every day, therefore, is the conscious founding of the destination, every day is the conscious attainment of the origin.

Also relevant to this passage is the fact that #51 LIVING ESSENCE and #58 DAWNING EXISTENCE are the first and last numbers, respectively, in the sequence of *QI NUMBERS* (see FIGURE 18: THE FU XI ARRANGEMENT OF THE HEXAGRAMS, Book II, Part I, Chapter V, Section 8).

> *6. They journeyed within, exploring the different realms of human nature and Spirit—in this way, they were able to commune with the Oracle and follow the PATH OF FREEDOM. This they took from the hexagram MOVING SOURCE.*

Commentary

Hexagram #48 MOVING SOURCE comprises the trigrams Wind over Water, suggesting a time of Mystery within and Adaptation without. Here, the spiritual path of the *dream-body* is expressed in terms of the combination of *The Unknown* within and a profound integration into the *Great Mystery* without. Wind over Water: the fluidity of air without and the fluidity of water within, the wind-spirit without and the water-spirit within—two great Currents flowing together, spirit and matter, soul and body, a well of benefit moving through the spiritual landscape with unstudied grace and ease.

Letting slip the bonds of *personal identity*, awareness moves along with CONSCIOUS CHANGE as it carries nature and spirit into the metamorphic.

> 7. *They sent forth their intentions in order to make their work known in other times and places—in this way, they were able to collaborate with others of like mind. This they took from the hexagram* ATTRACTING ALLIES.

Commentary

Hexagram #11 ATTRACTING ALLIES comprises the trigrams Lake over Lightning, suggesting a time of inner Inspiration and outer Communion. Those who are driven within to perfect their work create ripples in the *intentional field* that capture the attention of others of like heart-mind. Spirits gather to the light of inspiration. *Magnanimous Qi* is the outpouring of intent that aims to benefit all, the collective work of *allies-at-a-distance* transcends culture and the generations: how can the helping spirits of eternity not come to assist their noble-hearted allies?

> 8. *They cultivated the circulation of* BENEFIT *among all things, seeking the best for all at the same time—in this way, they were able to keep vigil at the gate of* NEED *and address each appearance before its seed could take root and grow. This they took from the hexagram* UNIFYING INSPIRATION.

Commentary

Hexagram #10 UNIFYING INSPIRATION is composed of the trigrams Lightning over Moon, suggesting a time of inner Completion and outer Inspiration. When people are fulfilled and content, their inner work accomplished, they cannot help but inspire and encourage others in their own endeavors. Because they have untied their own knots, they are able to recognize the knots in others' lives. It is not simply that the wise share the benefit they have received—it is that human beings are one. It is not simply that human beings are one—it is that human beings and nature and spirit are different facets of the same diamond that is the World Soul. *Need* is a calling out into the valley of spirit and *benefit* is its echo. Spirit warriors are not deaf to this calling nor so poor in spirit that they cannot give of their treasure—an act that actually increases their own allotment of *benefit* rather than depleting it in any way. *Benefit* is *magnanimous qi* and *need* is a deficiency of *magnanimous qi*.

The community of human beings is utterly dependent on the free circulation of *benefit* for its well-being, just as the greater community of nature, human nature, and spirit cannot abide in harmonious balance without the community of human beings accomplishing its own inner work.

Spirit abhors a vacuum. Where *benefit* is lacking, *benefit* rushes in. The way in which *qi* is transmuted into ever finer and more sublime manifestations is an open secret: The baser drives are fired continuously with the *intent of benefiting all at the same time* until the metamorphic drive of the philosopher's stone is fully realized.

> *9. They trained themselves to cut off the past and future in order to fix their awareness on the mind moment—in this way, they were able to channel their creative will into actions that express the sacred nature of humanity's relationship with Nature and Spirit. This they took from the hexagram* CONCENTRATING ATTENTION.

Commentary

Hexagram #13 CONCENTRATING ATTENTION comprises the trigrams Lightning over Mountain, suggesting a time of inner Stillness and outer Inspiration. The ancients recognized that the outer flow of events through space creates the illusion of time, which human nature tries to internalize as an inner passage from past to future. This is an inference drawn from, not a direct perception of, awareness: when the light of awareness is turned back around upon itself, it clearly perceives its own non-temporal and non-spatial nature. The illusion of awareness passing through time is no more real than the clouds floating on the surface of a still pool—beneath the bright but sterile reflection of the sky, the depths of the pool teem with the mystery of life. Similarly, once we strip away the delusion of a *past behind* and a *future ahead*, there is not even the concept of a *present here*—there is simply this mind moment focused entirely on *what-presents-itself*. Instead of creating narratives of the past or future that justify behaviors and feelings that separate us from other people, nature, or spirit, we experience *what-presents-itself* in all its chrystaline purity, devoid of history, promise, or threat: *concentrating attention* is, in this sense, like a lightning-bolt striking the peak of a great mountain, where the lowest point of heaven touches the highest point of earth—where the lightning-bolt of attention touches the peak of momentary experience.

In this union of *what-opens-itself* and *what-presents-itself* lies the creative spirit of those who abide in the One Generation: without ancestors or descendants, those who embody the eternal marriage of awareness and creative intent are the living expression of the sacred marriage of Nature and Spirit. For this reason, *concentrating attention* is said to form the entire length of the road of *living potential*.

> *10. They honored their passions as gifts from the CREATIVE FORCES—in this way, they were able to train the wild nature of human being without breaking its spirit. This they took from the hexagram WIELDING PASSION.*

Commentary

Hexagram #23 WIELDING PASSION is composed of the trigrams Fire over Lake, suggesting a time of inner Communion and outer Understanding. Ascetics fail to live lives fully human, hedonists fail to live lives fully divine—how can either approach be considered in accord with the lifeway of *living potential*? The wild untamed passions of human nature are the source of wonder, awe, and curiosity: what autonomous forces well up in us, possess us for a while, and then depart to leave us wrung out and empty? To step into a human body is to steep oneself in the eternal quest: *What kind of being am I creating?* It is to step into the *already-made* and to take the reins of a mount with inclinations all its own. Too light a hand on the reins and the mount runs itself to death, too heavy a hand and we hobble its noble spirit—neither controlling nor being controlled by the body's ingrained habits, we revel in its soarings and its plungings, rider and mount one creative spirit at play in the greater passions uniting the Creative Forces in the ongoing *Act of Creation*.

> *11. They lived in harmony with NATURE, building their towns and cities into the landscape so that they flowed like wind and water on the land—in this way, they were able to form communities that sprouted from the land like living forests of light. This they took from the hexagram RADIATING INTENT.*

Commentary

Hexagram #25 RADIATING INTENT is composed of the trigrams Lightning over Sun, suggesting a time of inner Creation and outer Inspiration.

When the inner well of the creative spirit overflows into the outer landscape of inspired action, the community of noble-hearted men, women, and children emanate a single intent—that they live in perfect harmony with nature, dwelling in peaceful coexistence with one another, nature, and spirit. Since ancient times, this intent has been called the *universal love of land and life*. The ancients demonstrated that when people love land-and-life, it loves them in return, welcoming them with open arms to find their niche in the lushness of creation. This is the timeless secret that the spiritual ancestors whisper in our ears, that without radiating this intent above our intent to build and produce, our lives fall into discord and our civilization into ruin.

> *12. They honored death and kept it close in order to pour forth gratitude for being part of a wondrous creation—in this way, they were able to greet everyone they met as a fellow spirit warrior likewise facing their own inevitable demise. This they took from the hexagram COMPELLING MOTIVE.*

Commentary

Hexagram #7 COMPELLING MOTIVE is composed of the trigrams Lake over Wind, suggesting a time of inner Adaptation and outer Communion. Responding to *what-presents-itself* in a timely and authentic manner brings us into closer intimacy with *what-hides-itself*. The closer to life we grow, the nearer the presence of death is felt. This is because *what-presents-itself* is not less opaque than *what-hides-itself*—life is no less a part of the *Great Mystery* than death. It is we who become transparent, not our circumstances. Experience becomes transparent only to the degree that we mirror *what-presents-itself* without distortion. The drive toward attunement with what is greater than ourselves is the preeminent motive behind human transformation—and no single matter among *what-presents-itself* compels us to seek that attunement more than *what-hides-itself*. Mortality drives us to seek immortality, death drives us to seek the deathless. Our communion with *what-presents-itself* brings us into closer intimacy with those around us, pulling us closer to all facing their mortality with the courage and understanding at their disposal. This is the bond of the lifeway of *Flower-and-Song* presented in Book II, Chapter 11, Section 1 (pg 89).

> *13. They developed language in order to pass on what they had learned to the coming generations—in this way, they were able to materially assist the metamorphosis of their descendants. This they took from the hexagram REVEALING KNOWLEDGE.*

Commentary

Hexagram #24 REVEALING KNOWLEDGE comprises the trigrams Lake over Sun, suggesting a time of inner Creation and outer Communion. The ancients faced a dilemma, whether to transmit the *Open Secret* of transmutation or trust that everyone would discover the way on their own. Consulting the Oracle, they foresaw the trend of civilization as it was to pass through a time of spiritual darkness. For this reason, they devised a language of symbols that do not explain or describe the *Great Mystery* but do express it. To those who commune with the *living dream* of the *World Soul*, the language of transmutation is bright and clear as the sun in a cloudless sky.

From the first times, the universal blessing has ever been: *Awaken Early, Find Lifelong Allies.*

Chapter III. *The Power of the Hexagrams*

1. When a bubble pops, the illusion of inside and outside is suddenly apparent. Yet, while the bubble exists, the reality of inside and outside, no matter how temporary, is certain. Seen this way, the generative energy circulating among all things is certainly inside and outside every entity, no matter how temporarily. The HEXAGRAMS reveal the sixty-four possible combinations of the eight archetypes of internal and external generative energy.

Commentary

The power of the hexagrams lies in their capacity to reflect the internal and external states of change of any entity—whether an individual, organization, nation, or civilization itself—at any given moment. This section reminds us of the difference between the absolute and relative realms—that Change itself is absolute, for it never ceases, but its phases, as it passes through time, are relative. The meshing of these inner and outer phases of change produces the experience of peace and conflict, harmony and discord, security and insecurity, abundance and want. By concentrating on the flux of *qi* as it *manifests intent* in the passage of time, spirit warriors experience inner and outer states as *changes of intent*, which are, therefore, amenable to the influence of other intent. For this reason, inner states are open to influence from without, just as outer states are open to influence from within. Opening and closing the gate to *influencing-the-outer* and *being-influenced-from-without* is the secret art of employing the power of the hexagrams.

2. The field of action lies in the tension and harmony between the inner and outer forces of each HEXAGRAM. This interaction gives the HEXAGRAMS their meaning as SITUATIONS within which individuals must orient themselves and work to respond to circumstances with impeccable authenticity.

Commentary

The passage of time brings about tension and the resolution-of-tension in unending cycles at each and every stage of development. Likewise, times of harmony and peace are the seedbed of friction and rising tension. Because our inner and outer states of change are *intentional states*, they are open to our intention to either change or remain the same.

To respond to circumstances as they arise is to keep our minds clear of distracting thoughts, emotions, and memories in order to concentrate our attention on the clearest intent possible.

Intent is not simply a thought or feeling or wish or desire. It is a full-fledged *envisioning* that is both the child of *conscious imagination* and the parent of our ethical connection to the world. We do not merely dream awake—we dream within the greater waking of the World Soul. The external states of change we encounter are not purely accidental—they are the accumulation of many people's intents that have accreted to the eight archetypes over the course of millennia. These collective intents have a weight and momentum of their own: our individual intent cannot move them in another direction unless we are able to add the weight of the World Soul's intent to our own. This is why it has long been said that the most important aspect of the spirit warrior's training is aligning our individual intent with the intent of THE ONE. With practice, it is clear that there is no reason that all should not benefit at the same time—as this worldview takes root in the body's cells and the soul's memories, there is not even a hairs-breadth's distance between individual intent and the intent of the World Soul. With this accord, there is no mountain or star or historical momentum that might not be moved if such were its authentic *need*.

The internal state of change, too, is a collective intent, a largely unconscious accumulation of the familial and cultural intents we have internalized with the eight archetypes. It is for this reason that spirit warriors do not identify with the inner state of change any more than with the outer: pure radiant awareness, situated in the mind-moment of undifferentiated experience, holds its position *between the upper and lower trigrams* in order to promote their harmony, resolve their unavoidable tensions, and avoid their avoidable frictions. This is the spirit warrior's way of using the power of the hexagrams to maintain equanimity in the midst of change by following the current of good fortune.

> 3. *The way in which an entity experiences internal or external change is marked by the* LINE CHANGES *and the new* HEXAGRAM *constructed thereby. As bridges between the present* SITUATION *and the developing* SITUATION, *the* LINE CHANGES *trace the current trends that make up the actual transitions into the coming* SITUATION.

Commentary

The power of the hexagrams extends into the future by dint of their capacity to identify the predictable transformations of *qi* over time.

This is particularly apparent in the progression of the line changes within each of the six stages (See Book II, Chapter III, Section 3). Line changes in the first, second, and third stages result in internal changes of intent as marked by changes in the lower trigram. Line changes in the fourth, fifth, and sixth stages result in external changes of intent as marked by changes in the upper trigram. It is for this reason that the line changes are said to drive the transformation of the hexagrams: Changes among the six stages of development trigger changes in the internal and external states of intent, which produce the future SITUATION.

By way of example, line changes in the 2nd, 3rd, 4th and 6th places of Hexagram #33, below, produce Hexagram #35. Representing the present situation in this case is Hexagram #33 Accepting Instruction which, through its four line changes, develops into the future situation represented by Hexagram #35 Holding Back. The upper trigram has changed from Lightning (in Hexagram #33) to Mountain (in Hexagram #35). Likewise, the lower trigram has changed from Fire (Hexagram #33) to Lake (Hexagram #35).

4. It is here, in the confluence of the TRIGRAM interaction and the changing LINES, that the predictive power of the HEXAGRAMS reveals itself. The LINE CHANGES open and close the six stages and the inner and outer TRIGRAMS transform in turn, tracing the way of restoration and overthrow among the HEXAGRAMS.

Commentary

For effecting restoration, there is no greater power than the changing broken line. For effecting overthrow, there is no greater power than the changing solid line. This is the secret power of the hexagrams, which mirrors the intent of the World Soul and its *ethics of benefit* that ever restores what is valuable and overthrows what is harmful.

1. Just as NATURE is the visible half of SPIRIT, SPIRIT the invisible half of NATURE. And like NATURE, SPIRIT abhors a vacuum: Spirit warriors quell their hearts and empty their minds so that SPIRIT might rush in to fill the INNER VOID.

What is the cause of suffering in the world? People believing they are their bodies—and treating others as if they are their bodies. Spirit warriors train themselves to see everything and everyone as sacred spiritual persons, mysterious entities of unknown power for good.

Quelling the heart of all its fires, emptying the mind of all its preconceptions, spirit warriors arrive at the center of the COMPASS OF CHANGE, where they may pivot at will into the eight directions of generative energy without ever leaving the STILLPOINT.

Commentary

Creating a lodging-place for the One Spirit: such is the *Way of the Inner Void*. How many excuses there are for being distracted from true meaning! How many reasons there are to justify volatility and distress! The way of filling the heart-mind with troubling thoughts, emotions, and memories leads neither to plentitude nor self-sufficiency. The home of good fortune, on the other hand, is found at every step along the *path of mental fasting*.

This section reaffirms the relationship between the spirit warrior and the World Soul. Trying to preserve a continuity of personal identity by maintaining a constant recitation of thoughts, emotions, and memories centered around the body's experiences—this is not the way to true personhood or authentic fulfillment. Grasping the truth of the soul on the most fundamental level, that true and immortal identity does not reside with the body, spirit warriors train their bodies to abide in mental and emotional stillness so that the soul's thoughts, emotions, and memories might dissipate the fog that accrues between lifetimes: Understanding floods into the heart-minds of all who allow the dam of fear to break and empty out the reservoir of aloneness.

This communion with the soul awakens the body to its true efficacy, aligning its *qi* with the *Current of Good Fortune*. From ancient times, this is called *exhaling with the wind* and is thought of as blowing one's breath out into the same direction as the wind is blowing.

Moving with the *wind and water of qi*, spontaneously responding to inner and outer states with ease and grace, spirit warriors become wells of benefit, individual theophanies of the sacred marriage of *Nature and Spirit*.

For the *Compass of Change* referred to above, See FIGURE I: THE PRIMAL ARRANGEMENT, Part I, Chapter II, Section 3.

2. The higher soul relies on the senses of the lower soul to perceive the world of matter and participate in it. Only by voluntarily emptying itself of its habits of thought, emotion and memory can the lower soul perceive the world of sprit and participate in it.

The bridge uniting the world of matter and the world of spirit is generative energy. In the world of spirit it is INTENTION. In the world of matter it is FORM. The continuity of change within the world of matter depends on the categories of INTENTION in the world of spirit. The eight TRIGRAMS are the symbols of the categories of INTENTION that manifest as the individual phenomena in the world of FORM.

Commentary

As described in Chapter I, Section 9, above, the communion between the higher soul and the lower soul is essential to marrying this lifetime with the deathless self—a practice called *uniting the born and the unborn*. All that is born, of course, must die, just as all that is unborn cannot die. The higher soul, then, is part and parcel of the uncreated Being that has forever existed—it precedes all of creation, entering its different manifestations in order to transmute matter into life and life into soul. The senses of the higher soul are attuned to higher dimensions of spirit and so can only experience this world fully through a sublime integration of the body's senses. Such an integration is made impossible by the incessant stream of thoughts, emotions, and memories that passes for ordinary consciousness in the lives of those not exposed to the teachings of inner quietude. In order for the sublime marriage to be consummated, therefore, the lower soul, as the sum of the body's experiences, has to seek inner quietude voluntarily—it cannot be stilled until it is genuinely and authentically exhausted by its mental racing about. It is for this reason that it is said that *mental fasting is a higher hunger*.

The relationship between the higher soul and lower soul is of such importance that there is an entire esoteric branch of divination dedicated to its investigation and evolution. In it, the upper trigram represents the archetypal *season of the higher soul*, whereas the lower trigram represents the archetypal *season of the lower soul*. Spirit warriors make use of this form of the Oracle in order to focus their attention on the spiritual embryo developing from the marriage of the two souls.

The more sublime senses of the higher soul register the archetypal essences underlying form and phenomena in the world of the five senses. Generative energy, or *qi*, is the universal ether which, when condensed, manifests as matter and, when refined, manifests as spirit. In order for the world of matter and life not to go falling into constant random change of form, *qi* is self-organizing—beneath the profusion of forms in the world, *qi* maintains continuity of change by holding to the eight archetypes in the *order of completion*. Without the archetypes of universal intent carrying *qi* from creation to completion, there would be nothing to hold substance to form through all its transformations. This is the quintessential function of the PATTERN OF ORDER AND CHANCE, for randomness without structure is lifeless chaos, just as structure without randomness is spiritless predetermination.

> *3. The spiritual rhythm of creation lies in its tides of waxing and waning generative energy. Spirit warriors step back and open themselves to new experience when the tide wanes—they step forward and pour out new expression when the tide waxes.*
>
> *The waxing* TRIGRAMS *are* LIGHTNING, WATER *and* MOUNTAIN. *The waning* TRIGRAMS *are* WIND, FIRE *and* LAKE. *Spirit warriors follow the waxing generative energy forward to the* SUN *of creative power— they follow the waning generative energy back to the* MOON *of reflective tranquility.*
>
> *Making the eight* TRIGRAMS *their senses, spirit warriors see into the world of harmonious intent underlying the world of matter and shaping its events. They move with the waxing and waning tides of generative energy, arriving at opportunities before they present themselves and departing before disasters occur. They match the outer* TRIGRAM *by responding with the appropriate inner* TRIGRAM, *living a profoundly meaningful life that enriches all they touch.*

Commentary

Qi rises and falls, producing night and day, the seasons of the year, the phases of the moon, and the tides of the sea.

In human nature, these correspond to periods of rest and activity, growth and decay, expansion and contraction, and high and low moods. Timing our personal actions and intentions to coincide with the greater waxing and waning of generative energy is key to realizing good fortune. When opportunities are contracting, spirit warriors adopt a receptive attitude, opening their heart-minds to compassion for people and nature: seeking the low and empty places where *need* has yet to be filled, they find inspiration for their next endeavor. When opportunities are expanding, they adopt a creative attitude, giving form and substance to their compassion for people and nature: finding the necessary and unexpected places into which to pour *benefit*, they seek to pool resources and share responsibilities with others of like mind and temperament.

Essence recognizes essence: Good fortune relies on clear perception, interpretation, and intent—by internalizing the eight archetypes of the natural manifestation of *qi*, spirit warriors recognize the pattern of *qi* at work beneath the surface of appearances, interpret its direction and momentum accurately, and align their intent with its own. By perceiving the world-of-archetypes through their own sensory-archetypes, spirit warriors are able to accord with the rising and falling of *qi*: Their personal trigrams, in other words, snap to those of the greater trigrams in much the same manner as two magnets snap together spontaneously and of one accord.

Chapter V. *The Power of the Line Changes*

1. The Oracle whispers: "The window of opportunity opens—the influence you feel between you and your companions is felt by them, too. This heartfelt bond allows you all to move as one. You will achieve your goal but it will not be as fulfilling as expected."

Of old it has been said that there is One Mind. All other beings, both animate and inanimate, have transcended alienation and aloneness by embodying the unitary nature of the One Mind. Human nature alone remains to awaken to the all-at-onceness of the One Body giving Form to the Formless.

<u>Commentary</u>

Nothing is more mysterious than the way that the line changes transform the present hexagram into the future hexagram (see Book II, Chapter III, Section 3). This is because the line changes lie at the very crux of change, where archetypes shape-shift into other archetypes. This is a deep and dark place, hidden from the view of ordinary consciousness, a place that is at once lush and desolate, high and low, hot and cold, shining and shadowed. Giants move there and our ego-identities, dwarfed and awed by the ageless suprapersonal nature of those archetypes, seek safety in numbers by a social compact that agrees to speak only of what the ego-identity can grasp.

For the Oracle, who soars above that primordial landscape like an even more ancient being, this *changing* of the archetypes can only be synchronous—how can there be a past, present, or future when the Oracle dwells outside time? The line changes generate a new hexagram out of the old one but all this happens at the same from the Oracle's perspective. For human nature, dwelling inside time, this *changing* from one situation to the next follows the arrow of time from the present into the future. The power of the line changes lies in their incipient nature, which reaches a *tipping point of reversal* that incites archetypes to replace one another.

This section opens by reciting the Oracle's pronouncement for the fourth line change of Hexagram 36 STABILIZING COMMUNION. This line is at the bottom of the upper trigram, Lake, which speaks to its sense of responsibility among close allies. The lower trigram, Mountain, though, provides an inner sense of holding back even from such a rewarding situation. Overall, the hexagram teaches that even fellowship, empathy, and affinity among people does not fulfill our deepest longing for belonging: The raindrop seeks its destiny in its return to the sea.

Civilization's alienation from nature mirrors its alienation from spirit. The encapsulation of self in the form of an individual identity obstructs people from experiencing the greater sense of self that identifies with being part of the One Mind. Spirit warriors are those men and women who consciously allow their sense of individual self to be eclipsed by their post-individual self, the first-hand experience of which opens the floodgates of universal communion. All other entities in Creation are immersed in the One Being, existing in the harmony of life arising out of death—human nature alone holds itself apart from the Grand Unity. There is, however, an age-old lineage of wise women and wise men who tread the path of daring: striking out for the further horizon, they encompass all within their heart-minds. The ongoing renewal of all Creation beckons pioneers onward past every new frontier—this is the way all is explored and returned to the One. Of this lineage all that might be said is that it will continue to grow in number and influence until it, itself, becomes the *tipping point of reversal* that returns civilization to its state of unity with nature and spirit.

2. The great oak tree embracing the field between its branches above and roots below: it looks nothing like the acorn from which it springs. The beloved child embraced by its parents: it looks nothing like the sperm and egg from which it springs. Yet it is oak trees that produce acorns and human beings that produce sperm and egg.

Commentary

The ends of things do not look like their beginnings. The beginnings of things do not look like their ends. An acorn falling on a plain grows into a very different oak tree than one falling among rocks on a cliff face, even though they both come from the same tree. Likewise, one brother may grow up to be a beloved saint while the other grows into a hardened criminal, even though they are identical twins raised in the same home.

What changes are wrought between beginning and end? This is the power of the line changes.

3. Form and Formless are not two things. Lightning and Thunder are one. Idea and Realization cannot be pulled apart.

Commentary

The broken lines inevitably turn into solid lines. The solid lines inevitably turn into broken lines. Solid and broken lines are not two: they are always in a state of flux, like the seasons of the year or the cycles of the moon, now a bit more yang, now a bit more yin. The unchanging essence beneath appearances is the place of their synchrony and, thence, their communion.

> *4. Awakening to the One Mind occurs when human nature opens to the Universal Communion binding all Ideas together in the shared evolution of the Immediate Realization. Spirit warriors are those who do not hold themselves apart from all the other Ideas in the One Mind.*

Commentary

This section returns to the theme established in Section 1, above: Whereas the fourth line change of Hexagram 36 STABILIZING COMMUNION speaks to the longing for communion with the greater self, the hexagram itself points to just such a transpersonal communion. Recognizing that there is One Mind is the first step in the practice of Universal Communion. The second step is that of recognizing oneself as one of the individuated ideas within the One Mind. Full memory of this unique idea is a life-changing epiphany whereby one suddenly and irrevocably remembers one's true self. The third step is a thorough grasping of how one fits with all the ideas making up the One Mind. The fourth step, of course, is coming to grips with how one, as an embodied idea of the One Mind, manifests that idea in this lifetime. This, in its entirety, is the practice of *stabilizing communion*.

This unique idea *is* the higher soul. It is one's true and immortal identity within the One Mind. Just as one has a unique body within the physical universe, one has a unique meaning within the spiritual universe. And just as all the physical bodies in the universe are connected in a web of matter and energy, all the individuated ideas within the One Mind are connected in a web of awareness and intent.

To rediscover oneself as Idea is to step off the hundred-foot pole of doubt and return to the original homeland of Universal Communion. This is the context of the fourth line change of STABILIZING COMMUNION.

5. The Oracle whispers: "When people are given a futile task, they take it to heart and allow it to affect their self-confidence. Once you appreciate that it is infinitely better to fail at a futile task than an achievable one, you will regain your composure. Bring out your flexible half again—this is a test of character, not ability."

Of old it has been said that an untroubled spirit is untroubled no matter how difficult things are, whereas a troubled spirit is troubled no matter how good things are. Concentrating on what is absent drains us of generative energy, whereas concentrating on what is present replenishes our generative energy. Spirit warriors are those who are already happy.

Commentary

This section begins by reciting the Oracle's pronouncement for the third line change of Hexagram 46, HONORING CONTENTMENT. This line is at the top of the lower trigram, Water, which speaks to its sense of being isolated in the midst of uncertainty. The upper trigram, Lake, however, indicates that external circumstances are favorable, filled with joy and companionship. The overall situation is one of affinity, since the hexagram is made up of Lake above Water, elements that reinforce one another.

Though surrounded by uncertainty in the moment, the person drawing this line change ought to focus on the bigger picture, which is wholly benevolent in nature. *Honoring contentment* means, first and foremost, being content with contentment.

6. The Oracle whispers: "The search for peace of mind can itself become a source of anxiety and dissatisfaction. And it can lead to all kinds of questionable pursuits. The cornerstone of the inner sanctum is sincerity—if your heart is truly filled with the profound desire to find peace, then nothing can stand in your way."

Of old it has been said that human nature contains within itself the instinct to transcend instinct. The inner path leads to the inner landscape of the One Spirit. Enlightenment is the last trap of Illusion. Spirit warriors are those who let go of life when living and let go of death when dying.

Commentary

This section begins by reciting the Oracle's pronouncement for the sixth line change of Hexagram 44, REFINING INSTINCT. This line is at the top of the upper trigram, Lightning, which speaks to its sense of trying to disengage from unexpected developments. The lower trigram, Water, complicates matters by adding another level of inner uncertainty to the situation. The overall situation is favorable, since Lightning over Water indicates a storm that brings rain to the land: Though lightning strikes and thunder roars in the sky, the roots of the plants are nourished underground.

Where others might find themselves embroiled in the drama of events, the person drawing this line change disentangles herself or himself by maintaining the strongest intent to be of the most benefit to the most possible.

7. The Oracle whispers: "Taking advantage of others in any form causes them harm, even when your participation is indirect and unintentional. Set your will against any form of harming others since that will result in harm to yourself. Set aside self-interest and you will regain your momentum and direction."

Of old it has been said that the law of spiritual cause-and-effect rewards the noble-hearted. Return to your path the moment you recognize a lapse in generosity of thought. Spirit warriors are those who consistently embody goodwill toward all, regardless of circumstances.

Commentary

This section begins by reciting the Oracle's pronouncement for the first line change of Hexagram 26, DIGNIFYING AMBITION. This line is at the bottom of the lower trigram, Lightning, which speaks to its sense of vulnerability in the midst of surprising inner experiences. The upper trigram, Fire, provides a sense of security and stability among outer circumstances. Overall, the time is one of opening opportunities.

When opportunities present themselves, it can be difficult not to act on self-interest. The person drawing this line change, however, faces this ethical dilemma with wisdom and compassion, succeeding because he or she places cooperation above competition in every event.

8. The Oracle whispers: "Some elements of your personality go unquestioned, as if they were intrinsic and unalterable. This is wrong-headed—if you were taken at birth and raised in a faraway culture, your personality would be wholly different. Do not be stubborn—everyone else cannot be wrong and you right."

Of old it has been said that light fills an empty room. Radiant awareness fills the body. There is nowhere for the One to hide. Spirit warriors are those who remake a nest for the phoenix every morning.

Commentary

This section begins by reciting the Oracle's pronouncement for the sixth line change of Hexagram 26, DIGNIFYING AMBITION. This line is at the top of the upper trigram, Fire, which speaks to its sense of disengaging from convention, received wisdom, and personal opinion. The bottom trigram, Lightning, illuminates matters internally by calling forth new inspiring visions. The overall situation is favorable, since it opens up new opportunities.

Fire is so small compared to Lightning but we will hide our thunderbolt even from ourselves in order to present a flickering flame that is acceptable those around us. Departing from our true self and inner power, we take up unreasonable ideas and habitual reactions that trivialize our lives. The person drawing this line change keeps the *beginner's mind*, ever open to honest criticism and always quick to return to the Way.

9. The Oracle whispers: "The situation is auspicious—you are at the vanguard of sweeping changes that will benefit all but those you replace. The principal task for now is to brighten the emotional atmosphere and give everyone hope. Slow down—actually implementing the new will take a long time."

Of old it has been said that every change arrives like a season. Actions must accord with the generative energy of the season. Periods of expansion are followed by periods of consolidation. Periods of deprivation are followed by periods of bounty. Spirit warriors are those who sense winter's darkness at the summer solstice—and spring's blossoms at the autumnal equinox.

Commentary

This section begins by reciting the Oracle's pronouncement for the fifth line change of Hexagram 54, REPEATING TEST. This line is in the middle of the top trigram, Sun, which speaks to its sense of being empowered by a period of creativity. The lower trigram, Moon, points to an inner state of receptivity and self-reflection. The overall situation is favorable in the long run, since the power of Sun outside is balanced by the caring nature of Moon inside.

Occupying a position of power in the midst of powerful forces: the person drawing this line change has the capacity, temperament, and skill to remove wrongdoers from the scene. She or he is mindful of moving at the right time and in the right way, so good fortune is assured.

> *10. The Oracle whispers: "You must beware of creating a crisis just when everything is going right. By counting on the wrong person at this time you will betray the confidence of all the others who have placed their trust in you. A slip here will result in a long fall—make others prove they share your new priorities."*
>
> *Of old it has been said that nothing is more essential than closing up one's own gaps. Recognize self-defeating habits by the way they keep re-appearing. Spirit warriors are those who stop leaking generative energy.*

Commentary

This section begins by reciting the Oracle's pronouncement for the fourth line change of Hexagram 4, MIRRORING WISDOM. This line is at the bottom of the top trigram, Fire, which speaks to its sense of being responsible to knowing. The lower trigram, Wind, signifies a disposition toward patient perseverance. The overall situation is auspicious, since the Fire of understanding is fanned by the Wind of diligence: With discipline, knowledge is internalized and becomes wisdom.

Being responsible to knowing means that we cannot in good conscience act in a way that is not in accord with what we know. Because everything is one living being that provides benefit to all at the same time—no less than the World Soul provides physical, emotional, intellectual, and spiritual succor to all equally—there is no cause for alarm, worry, or anxiety.

Allowing others to unduly influence our thinking with their own preoccupations is a tragic mistake—and a tragic missed opportunity to influence them in a way that lifts their sight to the further horizon. Blocking the self-defeating thoughts of others before they reach our heart-mind is a necessary part of the practice of defeating our own self-defeating habits of thought, emotion, and memory.

> *11. The Oracle whispers: "Do not make your quest for security so important that it overshadows all other facets of your life. Those around you long to bask in the warmth of your light-hearted nature. You cannot prepare for every eventuality but you can make every moment count—fall back on your inner resources."*

> *Of old it has been said that hope is just as hopeless as fear, for they are merely two sides of the same coin of imagined absence. Wisdom does not involve learning anything new—it revolves around the act of remembering something old. Spirit warriors move back to their original position of trust in Creation.*

Commentary

This section begins by reciting the Oracle's pronouncement for the second line change of Hexagram 10, UNIFYING INSPIRATION. This line is in the middle of the lower trigram, Moon, which speaks to its sense of trusting the innate perfectibility of all things. The upper trigram, Lightning, signifies inspired action and intent. The overall situation is highly favorable, since Lightning over Moon indicates a bright vision brought to realization: When those who are content inspire others to contentment, great works are at hand.

Hope and fear miss the mark: being content with contentment is the arrow's true aim. Knowing that the road of life is fraught with difficulties inures us to disappointment and frustration—rather, it forms a bond among people everywhere, who comfort and assist one another when most needed. By focusing on what is present instead of what is absent, spirit warriors feel the loving-kindness of the World Soul buoying their alliance.

> *12. The Oracle whispers: "The window of opportunity opens—the pivot of constructive change is in the palm of your hand. Look at your own era as if for the first time and adapt the perennial message to the needs of the time. The season has arrived and the soil is prepared—yours is the role of sowing the seeds of light."*

Of old it has been said that one who stands in a deep hole can see in only one direction, whereas one who stands on a high peak can see in all directions. By this we can tell where another person stands. Spirit warriors are those who adopt multiple points of view in order to accord with the One.

Commentary

This section begins by reciting the Oracle's pronouncement for the first line change of Hexagram 43, GOING BEYOND. This line is at the bottom of the lower trigram, Lightning, which speaks to its sense of unconditional surrender to the irrational. The upper trigram, Moon, signifies the completion of another phase of experience. The overall situation is highly auspicious, since Moon over Lightning indicates a leap of creative purpose: the more sublime the ending, the more sublime the next beginning.

The personal identity is largely a matter of accident and fate, whereas the true self is a deathless and uncreated being. The personal identity is largely restricted to the experiences afforded by its body's senses, whereas the true self is the beginningless accumulation and integration of uncountable forms, bodies, and lives. The personal identity is largely shaped by its mortality, whereas the true self autonomously creates its immortality. Since ancient times, the formula of *THE CHANGES* is: *Freedom in every sense!*

> *13. The Oracle whispers "If you try collaborating with your peers, their petty goals drive you out of the group. If you try working along similar lines on your own, their petty insecurities pull you into the group. If they will not raise their goals, go on without them—do not allow them to trivialize your contribution."*

Of old it has been said that seeing in the dark of night is a rarer gift than seeing in the light of day. In the light of day all the differences and distinctions between things can be seen, whereas in the dark of night all differences and distinctions blend into an undifferentiated whole. Spirit warriors are those who cultivate both gifts.

Commentary

This section begins by reciting the Oracle's pronouncement for the third line of Hexagram 35, Holding Back. This line is at the top of the lower trigram, Lake, which speaks to its sense of possible loss of the valuable. The upper trigram, Mountain, signifies stopping something from happening.

The overall situation is positive but requires great care, since Mountain over Lake indicates halting the momentum of gain and loss in its tracks: Having what we want is not nearly so empowering as wanting what we have.

The wise see spiritually and act strategically. *Seeing spiritually* means seeing the essence of things that grants one both insight and foresight. *Acting strategically* means acting on the ability to recognize the difference between trustworthy and untrustworthy, between beneficial and malicious, elements one encounters. This is called *Seeing with both eyes*.

14. The Oracle whispers: "When renewal is exploited to provide an excuse for making self-serving changes, then others take an antagonistic position. No matter how it may be justified, if you take advantage of others, you undercut the very support you will need. Pretend to be more caring and generous until you are."

Of old it has been said that times of great transformation bring out the best and worst in people. If your upbringing and life experiences have not led you to a generosity of spirit, then begin cultivating it now by imitating others who already possess it. Spirit warriors are those who do not miss an opportunity to benefit others by improving their own character.

Commentary

This section begins by reciting the Oracle's pronouncement for the sixth line of Hexagram 5, RESTORING WHOLENESS. This line is at the top of the upper trigram, Wind, which speaks to its sense of detachment from the restorative process. The lower trigram, Lightning, signifies the force of vitality.

The overall situation is extremely positive, since Wind over Lightning indicates the curative power of the vital force, *qi*: This line change points to the personal healing that can be undertaken by those raised in emotionally distant circumstances.

Wholeness means *uncut*. *Restoring* means *returning to the original condition*. Emotional detachment has its place in the therapeutic process if one is the healer—a profound compassion, universal in nature, is embodied in a demeanor of neutral concern. Those afflicted by such detachment, however, find it difficult to empathize with others and so suffer greatly from an unnecessary loss of affection, closeness, and intimacy.

Real adaptation of *qi* to real-life circumstances requires an unflinching look into one's heart and making no excuses for any lack of generosity of spirit: ultimately, *restoring wholeness* means that it is possible to return immediately and spontaneously to our own original, uninjured, enlightened nature. It is said of the right determination that *The journey of a thousand miles is already accomplished before one takes the first step*.

Chapter VI. *The Power of THE CHANGES as a Whole*

1. PROVOKING CHANGE and SENSING CREATION form the keystone of the metamorphic power of THE CHANGES as a whole. PROVOKING CHANGE addresses the ending of things, providing a catharsis that transforms pent-up tensions into the energy required to undertake new beginnings. SENSING CREATION addresses the continuity of things, providing the communion between nature, human nature, and spirit that grounds the sustaining of Creation in the Universal Love preserving all that is valuable. The union of PROVOKING CHANGE and SENSING CREATION establishes the alternations of generative energy working through the sequence of the remaining pairs of hexagrams whereby the intent of the One emanates throughout every level of Creation. What knots endings and beginnings together and revels in the miraculous unfolding? The sacred within all.

Commentary

The first hexagram, PROVOKING CHANGE, arises from the last hexagram, SAFEGUARDING LIFE. The difficulty with developmental processes is that they tend toward unsatisfactory, even self-defeating, endings. This is the reason that the sequence begins with PROVOKING CHANGE: at the end of development, that which cannot be replaced is threatened by a stagnating equilibrium of forces and must be broken through if the process of renewal is to continue.

Just as PROVOKING CHANGE and SENSING CREATION are the first two hexagrams in the sequence, AWAKENING SELF-SUFFICIENCY AND SAFEGUARDING LIFE are the last two: They point to the fork in the road, where the decision must be made—are actions inspired by a deeply-ingrained sense of the miraculous nature of the sacred in everything or are they inspired by short-sighted self-interest and heartless materialism? Understanding this relationship between the first pair of hexagrams and the last pair of hexagrams in the sequence is key to interpreting the historical and cosmological meanings that extend beyond the more personal considerations.

2. The hexagrams point to the problem of self-defeating relationships that arise when power stagnates in unjust symmetries. The sequence of the hexagrams traces the path of the individual out of the Age of Darkness, pointing out the road of freedom whereby self-defeating power might be tamed by the Universal Civilizing Spirit.

Commentary

The hexagrams follow one another according to the law of spiritual cause-and-effect. Those who work their way through the sequence discover the *path of fate* to be a predictable series of action-and-backlash on the subliminal level of *qi*. Familiarity with the sequence heightens our sensitivity to the way we perceive, or are affected by, *qi* without our usually being aware of it. As we become more aware of the way that *qi* seeks to benefit all things at the same time, we see how the *will to dominance* dams the circulation of *qi*, leading to stagnation of creative renewal on every level. Following the sequence through all sixty-four hexagrams allows us to perceive the way in which fate pulls us along, depleting the vitality of our *qi* and boxing us into more and more predictable attitudes and behaviors. Casting the Oracle, however, permits us to step outside the sequence of hexagrams by means of the line changes—moving backward and forward within the sequence, we are able to step outside fate and reclaim our *freedom in every sense*. Such freedom is essential to casting off the chains of our *will to dominance* and making room in our heart-minds for all to share the very best at the same time. This is called *Taming human nature without breaking its sprit.*

3. THE CHANGES is an ocean wherein every drop of past and future and near and far is fused together in an indivisible spiritual whole. Essence calls to essence and receives an answer as if by echo. From the greatest to the smallest, all things are immediately connected in the radiant awareness of the Oracle.

Commentary

The Oracle stands outside time. Its being is synchronous, its awareness is all-at-once. Nothing, no matter how small or seemingly insignificant, can be destroyed without destroying all of Creation. Individuality is a bubble, a temporary membrane temporarily separating a temporary inside from a temporary outside—when the bubble bursts, what difference between the inside and the outside? The Oracle's path of freedom uncovers the metamorphosis of human nature.

4. THE CHANGES embraces THE ONE, mirroring THE WAY of the CREATIVE FORCES. Mystery leads to Knowing and Knowing leads to further Mystery. Lift a corner of the blanket and it is there to see all at once. Yet there is forever another blanket beneath. Illuminating one mystery, THE CHANGES uncovers a yet deeper one.

Good fortune in the end does not depend on learning or power—it depends on transforming endings and radiating bliss.

Commentary

The deepest mysteries are the closest to home. Who is it that knows? What is knowing? Is knowing perception or reflection? How can the senses register anything new, given that they are composed of the same material as the world they sense? How can anything new be known, given that the ideas of human nature are composed of the same pattern of archetypal forms as the world they conceive? If nothing new can be perceived or known, how is it that nothing changes? If it is a non-dual universe, how is it that we never change? What, then, is it that appears to change?

THE ONE does not distinguish between the absolute and relative realms. How *the unchanging* and *the changing* coexist can be known but not explained. THE WAY of the CREATIVE FORCES is an eternal unfolding of potential. How *the changing* perpetually renews itself at the well of *the unchanging* cannot be described but it can be expressed. The *living potential* of each being—the *innate perfectibility* of each Idea of THE ONE—is ouroboric: concerned with the knotting together of endings and beginnings, it finds the path of immortality, the path of the mind-flower, the path of the ecstatic life. Seeds of light give rise to blossoms of light, which in turn give rise to seeds of light, forever sowing the Ground of Being, the Great Mystery, with the light of mind that is at once the *knot of immortality* and the player of the *sacred game* of creation.

Chapter VII. *The Metamorphic Properties of Hexagrams*

1. THE CHANGES is handed down across the generations to keep alive the Universal Civilizing Spirit so that it might end the five thousand year Age of Darkness and bring forth the coming Age of peace and prospering for all.

Commentary

THE CHANGES is the discovery of the most observable elements of the subsensorial world around us. The trigrams, hexagrams, and their lines stand at the threshold of liminal knowing. They embody the borderland pattern of perception, where the conscious and unconscious are both structured by the imaginal, where nature and human nature are both informed by the World Soul. *This is the discovery of the imaginal by the imaginal.*

This exploration of the dream by the dream body cannot be conceived in terms of conscious and unconscious or of reality and imagination. This is because it is an exploration of Being that precedes Thinking, a self-reflexive *coming-to-know the Outer from Within.* Radiant awareness, the light of mind, explores the imaginal landscape of archetypes by exercising the subtle wind of pure intent to encounter the soul-making forces of creation and completion, of communion and aloneness, of knowing and mystery, of sudden and gradual. Before there are concepts of experience, there is experience—and before there is experience, there is the experiencer: before knowing, there is the knower, not a blank tablet of un-knowing but, rather, an archetypically-structured pattern of perception that makes knowing possible. This perceptive inventory, in the sense of registering perception, draws back the veil from the mythic nature of experience and allows for a re-emergence of full participation within it.

Not words but images—not the language of waking or the silence of sleeping but the reflections in the mirror of dreaming—are the emotion-laden forms of symbols uniting existence and essence. Great-souled beings scratched these images in the soil and inscribed them on the heart, finding in their archetypal nature the corresponding figures of heaven and earth, spirit and matter. They divined the ONE MIND and came to know the subtle wind of its pure intent: *How does awareness tame the body without breaking its spirit?* Following the ancient dictum, *As Within, So Without,* our spiritual ancestors established the Great Work, a long-range program of awakening human nature to its fullest potential by establishing schools propagating the wisdom teachings of *Freedom in every sense.*

By cultivating the understanding of self-transcendence, in the sense of *freedom even from what one most reveres*, the union of body and awareness, of existence and essence, was accomplished on an ever-widening field of individuals—all with a view toward making this individual realization universal. Axiomatic to the Great Work is the *principle of inevitability*: a lesser force subsumes a greater force when it adopts the direction and momentum of the whole as its own. According with the synergistic intent of the Whole, the Great Work embodies the Universal Civilizing Spirit of the World Soul. It is given to each generation to carry its torch forward, bringing its expression into *fittingness* with the historical age in which they live.

The Age of Darkness is passing. The archetypes are not solely the self-organizing path of fate—they are also the self-transcending path of freedom: the same archetypes that drive the collective to self-destruction also drive individuals to leap into *The Beyond* and make it their home. The post-individual communes spontaneously with nature, spirit, and other people. The community of post-individuals inevitably completes the Great Work. The transmutation of human nature is itself the philosopher's stone that initiates the further transmutation of nature and spirit.

> *2. RENEWING DEVOTION reaffirms our dedication to the first ancestor's vision. STAYING OPEN urges us to cultivate as wide a range of interests and relationships as possible. GOING BEYOND pushes us toward the limitless. FOSTERING SELF-SACRIFICE holds us to our vow to serve others. HOLDING BACK teaches us not to act on our first reaction. RESTORING WHOLENESS returns a forgotten part of ourselves. HONORING CONTENTMENT reminds us to treasure times of well-being. DEVELOPING POTENTIAL calls us to nurture invisible seeds. SUSTAINING RESILIENCE assures us that security and stability are gained not by material force, but by spiritual suppleness.*

<u>Commentary</u>

This and the following two sections focus on different aspects of nine hexagrams: HEXAGRAM 16 RENEWING DEVOTION, HEXAGRAM 49 STAYING OPEN, HEXAGRAM 43 GOING BEYOND, HEXAGRAM 6 FOSTERING SELF-SACRIFICE, HEXAGRAM 35 HOLDING BACK, HEXAGRAM 5 RESTORING WHOLENESS, HEXAGRAM 46 HONORING CONTENTMENT, HEXAGRAM 59 DEVELOPING POTENTIAL, AND HEXAGRAM 29 SUSTAINING RESILIENCE.

This first section addresses the conscious intent of each of these nine hexagrams.

3. RENEWING DEVOTION fosters sincerity that leads to contentment. STAYING OPEN fosters learning that expands future opportunities. GOING BEYOND fosters unconventional thinking that crosses every threshold. FOSTERING SELF-SACRIFICE fosters compassion that builds alliances. HOLDING BACK fosters patience that leads to the prize. RESTORING WHOLENESS fosters original nature that redeems acquired nature. HONORING CONTENTMENT fosters loving-kindness that radiates blessings. DEVELOPING POTENTIAL fosters trust that produces more than it consumes. SUSTAINING RESILIENCE fosters wisdom that endures all change.

Commentary

This second section addresses the unconscious intent of each of these nine hexagrams.

4. RENEWING DEVOTION responds with wonder in the face of essence. STAYING OPEN responds with calm in the face of experience. GOING BEYOND responds with drive in the face of existence. FOSTERING SELF-SACRIFICE responds with compromise in the face of upheaval. HOLDING BACK adopts stubbornness when treasuring. RESTORING WHOLENESS adopts adaptability when surprised. HONORING CONTENTMENT adopts joyfulness when overwhelmed. DEVELOPING POTENTIAL adopts inscrutability when progressing. SUSTAINING RESILIENCE responds with non-resistance in the face of resistance.

Commentary

This third section addresses the imaginal intent of each of these nine hexagrams.

Chapter VIII. *Revering the Lines*

1. THE CHANGES is a mirror
   of the world within you.
   It is the never-changing ever-changing:
   Taking turns occupying
   The six empty placeholders,
   Ascending and descending the secret ladder,
   Broken and unbroken rungs replace one another.
   They defy convention or dogma—
   They are charged with generative energy itself.

2. They reflect the rhythm of the seasons
      passing inside and outside.
   Looking inward or outward,
      they point to accord.

3. They trace the path of freedom.
   They teach the alchemy of benefit and need,
   The heirloom of your spiritual ancestors.

4. Sit with the Oracle in the room without walls—
   Attend with open heart-mind
      and the law of fate is laid bare.
   Those with cobwebs over their eyes, though,
      find it difficult to escape the trap.

Commentary

This chapter is divided into four verses that speak to the sacred nature of the lines.

The first verse states that THE CHANGES itself is the broken and solid lines in perpetual motion within the six stages of the hexagrams. Because these six stages of development do not just exist in the outer world but the inner world, as well, THE CHANGES is a mirror reflecting the never-changing ever-changing *qi* that is, at its heart, a profound magic. Generative energy is never-changing because it is the oceanic reservoir of undifferentiated potential that can neither be created nor destroyed—just as it is ever-changing because it constantly and forever transforms into all the possible manifestations of nature, human nature, and spirit within the flow of time.

See FIGURE 9: THE SIX STAGES OF THE HEXAGRAM, Book II, Chapter III, Section 3.

The second verse states that it is not just the six stages of development that are both within and without—it is the rhythm of change, as well. Inward or outward, it does not matter—change follows the same rhythm, which is counted in the measures of 6, 7, 8, and 9.

See FIGURE 8: THE INNER COMPASS, Book II, Chapter II, Section 4.

The third verse states that the line changes are the mechanism by which the Oracle is able to direct our attention to the Way of Freedom—rather than being carried along by the natural process of eventual decay reflected in the sequence of the 64 hexagrams, we are able to follow the line changes from one hexagram to another, moving back and forth within the sequence in accord with our participation in the *universal intent of benefit*. As our participation deepens, we are not simply responding to our own *need* by finding *benefit* in change—we increasingly move through the changes in order to respond to the *need* of others.

This verse also contains a reference to the secret practice of the ancients whereby the lead of *need* is transmuted into the gold of *benefit*.

The fourth verse states that the conventional path of life is a trap of fated illusion that can be escaped by listening to the wisdom teachings of THE ONE. The conventional path, the path of fate, is seen as a path of social control, one where the full potential of human nature is not encouraged. Rather, the traditional structuring of civilization has not changed appreciably for millennia—the separation of people according to wealth and privilege has lead to a wholly false picture of reality into which people are born and raised, unaware until their later years of the obvious alternatives under which they might have lived.

Despite the superficial changes in outward appearance, no culture in historical times—other than local societies of indigenous peoples—has formed a society of peers. Instead of establishing a civilization founded on teaching contentment, cooperation, and self-control, the conventional path leads people into a maze of culturally-accepted enticements, competition, and intimidation.

It is in this sense that it is said that the path of fate is the path of *leaking qi, or leaking generative energy*. The *creative genius* of human nature needs to be recognized and cultivated if it is to build on the great works of the ancients and carry forward their project of establishing a civilization of peace and prospering for all. When this genius within men, women, and children is shunted off into trivial distractions and meaningless make-work, society devolves into a stagnant pool of unconscious hopelessness and disempoweredness. Just as we are born into a universe of language that has already been created in full and to which we must adapt if we are to communicate with others, we are born into the path of convention that sweeps us along with its momentum toward the ultimate end of a disillusioned life. This is called *seeing with cobwebs over the eyes*: Such a one can see enough to get by in the world but cannot see the whole of its miraculous nature and boundless benevolence.

The Oracle teaches lessons by which *qi* is accumulated and cultivated in such a way that we store up *inner power* that can then be channeled by the *creative genius* into *acts of benefit*. By not wasting energy on trivial thoughts, emotions, memories, intentions, or reactions, we actually reverse the flow of *qi* by bringing in more and more as our active participation in the sacredness of everything increases. This focus on *meaningfulness* as a primary aspect of the Great Mystery provides the key to the *gate of gratitude*, through which passes the most refined essence of *qi*. Setting aside the trivial, picking up the valuable—*inner power* collects, pools, and intensifies, waiting for those moments when it might pour forth in the most harmonious and creative confluence with the intent of THE ONE.

The root of creativity is receptivity, so concentrating on the lessons of the Oracle requires a quiet abiding in a meditative state. This is called *sitting in the room without walls* and is not different than *gazing at the grey wall for nine years*. Out of this calm waiting comes understanding of the law of spiritual cause-and-effect binding the hexagrams into the sequence of the path of fate. Wiping away the cobwebs of illusion from their eyes, opening their heart-minds to the Oracle—in this manner, spirit warriors adopt the lessons appended to the hexagrams as their creative responses to the direction and momentum of fate.

The sequence of hexagrams, in other words, lays out the path of fate, while the lessons attached to them give the Oracle's advice as to how to transmute it into the path of freedom.

Chapter IX. *Tracing the Lines*

1. The lines of each hexagram express the emerging and submerging of issues. They speak to those stages of development requiring an increase or a decrease of attention. They are the bedrock of the hexagrams, pointing to where the focus of mind or resources should be directed. Their meanings are colored by the context of their hexagram, like each day is colored by its season.

Commentary

Seasons are made up of 90 days but they are more than the sum of their days—this is because there are other factors, such as the tilt of the earth on its axis and the global currents of the oceans, that determine the nature of each day. Likewise, hexagrams are made up of six lines but they are more than the sum of their lines—the interaction of their inner and outer trigrams is the primary factor determining the nature of each hexagram, which in turn provides the context within which their respective lines stand. Though there is no season without its 90 days, the character of those days is governed by the qualities of the season—just as there is no hexagram without its six lines but the character of those lines is governed by the qualities of the hexagram.

Each of the 64 hexagrams is made up of unchanging lines—of sevens and eights—and it is only when one or more of its lines is activated by a tension—by a six or nine—that the changing lines arise and resolve into a new hexagram: After an issue has been in the foreground of attention (seven) long enough (nine), it submerges into the background of attention (eight)—after an issue has been in the background of attention (eight) long enough (six), it emerges into the foreground of attention (seven). [See FIGURE 12: MARKING SHIFTS OF ATTENTION, Book II, Chapter III, Section 5]

While the lines making up the 64 hexagrams differ, the six stages of development are always the same. Whether concerning an individual, a relationship, a group, an institution, a nation, humankind, nature, or spirit itself, every situation contains the six stages of development. Not every stage is activated at the same time as a rule—generally, the issues of some stages are not requiring attention (eight) while others are (seven).

The following five sections describe the nature of the six stages of development. [See FIGURE 9: THE SIX STAGES OF THE HEXAGRAM, Book II, Chapter III, Section 3]

2. The bottom line refers to dependence and vulnerability. The top line refers to disentanglement and interdependence. They are like the stages of infant and elder within every person or institution. Their innate natures are considered to be represented by a solid line and a broken line, respectively, but their real-world correctness is actually determined by the context of their hexagram. In general, they do not play as active a role in the dynamics of the situation.

Commentary

The first and sixth stages of the hexagrams generally stand outside the action of the situation. They are thought of as entering and leaving the situation and so have, as a rule, less investment in its dynamics and outcome. That said, there are numerous exceptions, such as the first line of HEXAGRAM 1 PROVOKING CHANGE or the sixth line of HEXAGRAM 30 TRANSFORMING EXTINCTION. Leading into the situation, the first line is thought of as active, or an unbroken line, while the sixth line, leading out of the situation is thought of as withdrawing, or a broken line. These are traditional ways to consider how to interpret specific lines within specific hexagrams: Since half of all bottom lines are broken and half of all top lines are unbroken, it is possible to question whether their nature (broken or unbroken) is appropriate to their respective stage. Again, this is a rule of thumb that has many exceptions—this is because the dynamics of the hexagram as a whole are the determining factor of a line's *fittingness* to the time.

3. It is in the four inner lines that equalities and inequalities in the distribution of generative energy are expressed. Here the complex relationships between the stages of development work themselves out, creating the dynamics particular to each of the 64 situations.

Commentary

The four inner lines are the nucleus of the hexagram. They comprise, as a rule, the field of action wherein the give-and-take of *qi*—often manifested as power, resources, allies, affection, or good fortune—is played out.

4. Grasping the dynamics of the lines allows us to arrive ahead of time at the junctures of good fortune—and to depart ahead of time the crossroads of misfortune. Spirit warriors are those who internalize the lines and come to act through them without conscious deliberation.

Commentary

Spirit warriors know that they serve a purpose, even though they do not know what that purpose is. They can tell, however, when their path begins to veer away from that purpose—so they use this as their lodestone, always returning immediately to the correct heading. This is called *Being a master of the short return.* Making their own nature fluid and adaptable when fitting, firm and immovable when fitting—spirit warriors practice harmonizing their masculine and feminine halves until their actions and intentions are spontaneously in accord with THE ONE. This no different than the master musician who practices diligently in order to be able to improvise at will.

5. The second line refers to trust, the fourth line refers to responsibility. They are like the stages of middle childhood and early adulthood within every individual and organization. The second line is central to the lower trigram, therefore it typically carries greater weight. The fourth line is the bottom line of the upper trigram, therefore it typically carries lesser weight. Their innate natures are considered to be represented by a broken line but their real-world correctness is actually determined by the context of their hexagram.

Commentary

The second and fourth lines are both even and so thought of as broken lines—since half of all lines in the second and fourth stage are unbroken, this traditional way of determining the *fittingness* of those lines within specific hexagrams is superseded by the overall context of the hexagram.

6. The third line refers to separation and alienation. The fifth line refers to power and authority. They are like the stages of adolescence and full adulthood within every individual and organization. The third is the top line of the bottom trigram, therefore it typically carries less weight. The fifth line is the central line of the upper trigram, therefore it typically carries greater weight. Their innate natures are considered to be represented by a solid line but their real-world correctness is actually determined by the context of their hexagram.

<u>Commentary</u>

The third and fifth lines are both odd and so thought of as unbroken lines—since half of all lines in the second and fourth stage are broken, this traditional way of determining the *fittingness* of those lines within specific hexagrams is superseded by the overall context of the hexagram.

Chapter X. *The Lines in Eternity*

1. THE CHANGES spans time and distance, accompanying the generations of humanity on their journey to perfection. It embodies the Way of Spirit, the Way of Nature, and the Way of Human Nature in the three lines of the trigrams. The doubling of the trigrams produces the hexagrams, which embody these three primordial forms of generative energy in their bigrams. The six lines are the footprints of the never-changing ever-changing generative energy making its Way through the unfolding Creation.

Commentary

THE CHANGES is the great ally of humankind. It is a living voice of the World Soul that has not been stilled. It spoke to the ancients just as it speaks to us today. It reflects the intent of THE ONE, which is *to benefit all at the same time*. It is this intent that manifests as the *Seedbed of Creation*, within which thrive both butterflies and mosquitoes, both roses and ragweed. The road of perfection is one of mutual evolution, where all the best characteristics of each form are maintained in such a way that what benefits one does not cause a detriment to any other. The *intent of universal benefit*, in other words, is one of *innate perfectibility*—it is the methodical working out of all those relationships in which benefit for one is detrimental to another. The eventual destination of the journey of perfection is the natural disappearance of disease, parasitism, and other forms of competition among all. It does not imply the eradication or disappearance of species—rather, it means that all forms are adapting in such a way that they partake of the occanic reservoir of benefit without taking from any other form.

The same process is occurring within the social evolution of humankind. It is in this sense that the Oracle accompanies the generations on this journey, guiding them toward the goal of universal shared benefit through its perennial ethics of *inspired action*. The wisdom teachings embedded in *THE CHANGES*, in other words, embody the lessons of the emerging *Age of Peace and Prospering for All*, in which everyone benefits without causing harm or distress to any other.

It is for this reason that the six lines are experienced as living manifestations of *qi*. As they consolidate in archetypal forms, they illuminate the essential nature of the landscape of the situation—and when they change, they illuminate the incipient nature of mutual evolution and the overarching intent of THE ONE to bring all into harmonious balance. In this sense, each hexagram constitutes a *qualitative allotment of qi* and the sequence of 64 hexagrams establishes the proper distribution of *qi* that sustains the cycle of mutual evolution for the next turning of the Age in 5,125 years.

For the way spirit, nature, and human nature are embodied in the lines of the trigrams and hexagrams, see Book I, Chapter II, Section 4.

For a compendium of trigram attributes, see Book I, Chapter III, Section 11.

For the doubling of the trigrams into hexagrams, see Figure 18, Book II, Chapter V, Section 8.

> *2. The never-changing WAY manifests itself as an ever-changing cycle of remaking. The six stages of remaking are occupied by the coming and going of the CREATING AND SUSTAINING FORCES. Because the six stages embody real-world development, they give form to the dynamics of relationships within every individual and organization. Stages differ in needs so each possesses an innate nature. Between the interaction of the inner and outer trigrams, the nature of the broken and solid lines, and the issues of the six stages of a hexagram, the Oracle's message may be ascertained and the paths of fate and freedom revealed.*

Commentary

Within this Creation, nothing can be created or destroyed—it is all in the process of remaking. For this reason, it is called *The Already*. Our journey through *The Already* consists of taking what we find at-hand and fashioning it into the most meaningful lifetime possible. Each of us has, therefore, a lifework to achieve—not one to discover but one to fashion for ourselves, for that is the part of *The Already* that does not yet exist.

Qi manifests within human nature as a *developmental process of six stages*, the physical stages of which embody the life-lessons we need to master in our formation of character—

6th	elder	positive disengagement
5th	mature adulthood	authority, empowerment
4th	first adulthood	independence, responsibility
3rd	adolescent	alienation, separation
2nd	child	trust, bonding
1st	infant	vulnerability, dependence

The CREATING AND SUSTAINING FORCES are the masculine and feminine halves of *qi* and are represented as solid and broken lines that take turns occupying the six stages. Because *qi* builds up into states of tension that must be released in order to be resolved, its masculine and feminine halves are sometimes in states of tension and sometimes in states of resolution—

6	broken changing to solid	tension of background issue emerging to foreground
7	unchanging solid line	resolved issue in the foreground of attention
8	unchanging broken line	resolved issue in the background of attention
9	solid changing to broken	tension of foreground issue submerging to background

Issues arise and fall away, stabilize and are integrated into unconscious activity, fossilize and need to be broken open, provoke change and need to be integrated into conscious activity—the cyclical dynamic within each of the six stages, whereby issues are activated and resolved, opens a window on the deeper implications of their respective hexagrams.

Insight into the meaning of the hexagrams can be furthered by considering the interaction of their lower and upper, inner and outer, trigrams—

SUN:	Inner: ADVENTUROUS	Outer: CONTROVERSIAL
LAKE:	Inner: WELCOMING	Outer: ACCEPTED
FIRE:	Inner: CONFIDENT	Outer: DECISIVE
LIGHTNING:	Inner: RESOLUTE	Outer: TESTED
WIND:	Inner: INQUISITIVE	Outer: TEMPERED
WATER:	Inner: UNSURE	Outer: INDECISIVE
MOUNTAIN:	Inner: RESERVED	Outer: OBSTRUCTED
MOON:	Inner: ENCOURAGING	Outer: FULFILLED

These three factors, then—the issues of the six stages, the tension and resolution among the six lines, and the interaction between the inner and outer trigrams—constitute the structural elements contributing to the interpretation of a divination.

For the attributes of the six stages, see FIGURE 9: THE SIX STAGES OF THE HEXAGRAM, Book II, Chapter III, Section 3.

For the dynamics of tension and resolution between line, see FIGURE 12: MARKING THE SHIFTS OF ATTENTION, Book II, Chapter III, Section 5.

Chapter XI. *The Importance of Habits in THE CHANGES*

This is a work created at the end of the five thousand year cycle of the oppression of the human spirit. It reflects the return to a meaningful lifeway that honors human nature by bringing it back into accord with nature and spirit. For this reason, its focus is on the universal transition from a time of darkness to a time of light, recognizing that such a metamorphosis is initiated and sustained by the growing alliance of individuals undergoing that very transition within themselves. In a time when the self-defeating attitudes and behaviors of humanity are themselves being defeated, the focus of change falls upon the pivot of habit. The constellation of self-defeating habits of thought, emotion, and memory is the enemy-within, whether of an individual, group, or humanity as a whole. Spirit warriors are those who defeat the enemy-within by training themselves to embody a wholly beneficial repertoire of thoughts, emotions, and memories. This is a work embodying the wholly beneficial thoughts, emotions, and memories of our common spiritual ancestors.

Commentary

The miraculous nature of this Creation—and its unbounded Benevolence—does not blind us to the wrongdoing of those who usurp the *beneficial qi* at their disposal and turn it against other people, nature, and spirit. The nightmarish results of such malicious intent mar the potential beauty and harmony of the world right before our eyes—indeed, much of the Oracle's guidance through the *path of fate* pertains to recognizing and counteracting the residual ill will of the passing Age. The Age of Darkness was inevitable, it seems, the necessary passage through blind greed, ambition, and violence—as inevitable, to be sure, as the emerging Age of Light ushering in a long period of peace and prospering for all.

This emerging Age carries us into a new lifeway that embodies the incorruptible ethics of an inextinguishable worldview. These ethics are initially externalized into society by the vanguard of individuals embodying them and, in time, take root in the collective to supplant the previous lifeway of self-defeating intentions and actions. The pivot point of such a transformation lies, first, in the extinction of ingrained habits of perception and values and, second, in the creation of new, consciously accepted, habits of heart and mind.

The World Soul reveals itself in symbols, in the dream images of archetypal forms and relations between forms. It is *The Unconcealed* shaping the outer world of nature and the inner world of human nature in accord with its own eternal dream. This is the first language, the language of dreams that the sleeping unconscious first spoke to the waking conscious of earliest mankind. It is the oldest language, that of sun and moon, lightning and wind, fire and water, mountain and lake. And it is the language of art and magic that allows us to speak back to the World Soul and make our intent understood. Stepping back into the eternal dream of the World Soul, spirit warriors emerge, sudden as a bubble bursting, within the *Inner Landscape* of living images—this sacred space is no different than the world of Nature except that it is wholly manifest within the soul of Nature, for it is the dream body, the intentional body, of Nature. It is the Spirit of Nature, that holy center of the earth where Human Nature originated and is destined to return.

The World Soul speaks to us in images and it is through images that the World Soul understands us. This is the reason that spirit warriors cultivate the dream body, so that they might channel their inner power into acts of visualization whose images speak most clearly to the heart of the World Soul. The Way of the World Soul is to benefit all—but weeds will choke out more necessary plants, parasites will carry unnecessary diseases, and mean-spirited people will bring harm and discord to others. Those who purify their intent of self-interest and attune their senses to the archetypal images are able to speak to the World Soul in its own language, thereby making it aware of those places where *beneficial qi* has stagnated and is no longer circulating freely among all. This is called, *Calling out in the Mother Tongue to change the course of rivers.*

Words are an appendage to images—images have an existence prior to words. Those who speak to human beings, speak in words—those who speak to nature or spirit or the human soul, speak in images. The physical body is an appendage to the dream body—the dream body has an existence prior to the physical body. This is what is meant by the ancient saying, *What was your original self before your parents met?*

Chapter XII. *Recapitulation*

1. The Masculine Creative Force expresses itself in direct purposeful action. The Feminine Creative Force expresses itself in acts of unconditional nurturing. Neither behave in contrived or premeditated manners. They respond to changing circumstances with spontaneity, elegance, and ease. They treat all obstructions as the path and so nothing resists their advance.

Commentary

This final chapter provides a summary of the cosmology and mechanism of THE CHANGES.

The CREATIVE FORCES are the two halves of THE ONE. The masculine half is called *yang* and is represented in the hexagrams as a solid line. The feminine half is called *yin* and is represented in the hexagrams as a broken line. All of Creation, from the birth and death of stars to the arising and falling away of sensations, is the combination of *yang qi* and *yin qi*. This is the well of the living vital energy of THE ONE, whose overflowing of *benefit* bifurcates into the two rivers of *originating qi* and *sustaining qi*. All the possible combinations of their union produce the changing circumstances of the world—and those changing circumstances evoke in them further unions, which produce further changing circumstances. This ongoing act of creation embodies the PATTERN OF ORDER AND CHANCE, in that some changing circumstances follow the line of predictable cyclic changes and others follow the line of unpredictable onetime changes. Because the intent of THE ONE is transmutative, in the sense of opening the Way for the lower to become the higher, it does not conceive beforehand the end of its exploration. It cannot, therefore, act in any contrived or premeditated way but, rather, can only provide the alembic whereby everything might be distilled in the fire of their own intent.

2. The Masculine Creative Force is light-hearted and high-spirited in its pursuit of uncovering the already-perfect. The Feminine Creative Force is compassionate and caring in its pursuit of developing the becoming-perfect.

Commentary

The *innate perfectibility* of all things is the result of the union of the *already-perfect* and the *becoming perfect*. This what is meant by the saying, *The ordinary mind is a single thought away from the enlightened mind.*

The masculine half of the spirit warrior is a microcosm of the Masculine Creative Force at work in the macrocosm—its impulse drives it to discover the *already-perfect* within each moment of the microcosm, just as the Masculine Creative Force is driven to discover the *already-perfect* in the eternity of the macrocosm. Likewise, the feminine half of the spirit warrior is a microcosm of the Feminine Creative Force at work in the macrocosm—its benevolence waters every seed of *innate perfectibility* within the microcosm, just as the Feminine Creative Force draws the time-bound *becoming-perfect* macrocosm toward its eternal destination.

> *3. Line changes trace the path of generative energy as hexagrams change from one to another. The changing lines animate action in response to the dynamics of each situation. The window of opportunity opens for those of beneficial intent, closes for those greedy and self-serving. Change produces foresigns, just as a ship produces a prow wake ahead of itself. The lines are the foresigns of change, the trends developing into a new situation. The Oracle interprets the foresigns and points to the path of good fortune.*

Commentary

The 64 hexagrams embody the possible archetypal distributions of *yang qi* and *yin qi* in their combinations of solid and broken lines. The line changes depict the incipient tension and resolution of issues within the developmental stages of the hexagrams. These incipiencies are the foresigns of change, the harbingers of the synergistic developments underway beneath the surface of appearances. Those who would consult the Oracle in order to do evil find nothing in it of use, while those seeking to advance the cause of peace and prospering for all the Oracle treats as peers and companions on the Way.

> *4. Spirit is the invisible half of Nature. Nature is the visible half of Spirit. This the WAY of THE ONE. Human nature follows the Way and, like all of Creation, is half-Nature and half-Spirit. Spirit warriors are those at home between the land and the sky. They form an alliance with others of like spirit in order to further the work of the Universal Civilizing Spirit.*

Commentary

Matter is spirit. Form is the Formless. All of Creation is a single Being-of-nonduality within the single seed of Becoming-through-duality. Radiant awareness, as the living light illuminating the living mystery of night, is free of the entanglements of conceptions and so does not identify with either.

The spirit warrior passes through the realm of nonduality and the realm of duality without ever dwelling in either. It is for this reason that it is said, *Spirit warriors are free even of what they revere.* Understanding that all of Creation is a *Sacred Game* of unfathomable depth and significance, spirit warriors embody all the passion, skill, and originality by which great-souled players of every Age contribute to the defeat of the *enemy-within* and the triumph of *universal benefit.*

> 5. *Generative energy flows through the eight trigrams of Nature and the eight trigrams of Spirit, as well. Generative energy flows through the eight trigrams of humankind's inner nature and its outer nature, as well. Generative energy has an intent but it is not to benefit one at the expense of the many. Spirit warriors are those who make use of their own inner and outer nature in order to harmonize with the generative energy of Spirit and Nature.*

Commentary

The effort to connect the symbols of the dream body with the circumstances surrounding oneself can be frustrating. Likewise, trying to recognize the dream body's symbols and bring them into accord with those of the World Soul is a matter of evolving insight and sensitivity. In this sense, one's outer nature embodies one's relationship with circumstances, while one's inner nature embodies one's relationship with the World Soul.

The training of spirit warriors entails increasing their sensitivity to the archetypal images of *qi* so that they clearly reflect the symbols within circumstances and the World Soul. The archetypal nature of those symbols is embodied in the eight trigrams, which spirit warriors use to bring the images of their own dream body into harmonious balance with all. With practice, this mirroring of inner and outer realms reduces wasted effort in life, as if all the tumblers in a combination lock fell into place at the same time.

> 6. *Change follows its foresigns, just as a ship follows its prow wake, and new opportunities for gain and loss arise. Spirit warriors are those who know that they follow in the prow wake of their own intent. They keep close watch on their intentions, seeking to harmonize with their surroundings by sharing gain and keeping loss at bay. Throughout this work the lesson is the same: the greatest success comes to those who benefit all.*

Commentary

Change is magic, the most miraculous and mysterious of all things. It is the driving force behind time, entropy, and evolution. It causes things that are essentially one—like matter, or like psyche—to continually morph into different forms and identities. Change is the Open Secret, the *hidden intent* of THE ONE that is everywhere continually in the act of *unconcealment*. The trigrams and line changes embody *states of change*, which is to say, *incipient intent*, or *seeds of qi* that have not yet burst through the surface of appearances. Thorough investigation of the intent of change reveals the path of good fortune: *Benefit abhors a vacuum*. Those who empty themselves by constantly benefiting others are constantly being filled to overflowing from the universal well of *beneficial qi*.

> 7. *The intent of those seeking easy gain is hungry. The intent of those seeking security is anxious. The intent of those seeking the best for all immediately is open-handed. The intent of a troubled spirit is dire, the intent of an untroubled spirit is uplifting. Spirit warriors are those whose uninterrupted intent is peace and prospering for all.*

Commentary

The many kinds of people are driven by their different intents. Aligning oneself with people of like intent produces misfortune if that shared intent is one of self-interest. Forming alliances with other spirit warriors produces good works and leads to the inevitable Golden Age of Humanity.

Discerning the intent of others is essential to the act of forming alliances. What is meant by *people* applies to all, whether they currently have a physical body or not. Keeping one's own intent free of self-interest makes one repulsive to undesirable allies. The noble-hearted do not attract the ignoble—nor do they allow themselves to be attracted to the ignoble.

With this section, the second volume of this work comes to a close, its admonitions the Oracle's *speaking* the Universal Civilizing Spirit: *The whole of THE CHANGES is a matter of transmuting human nature*.

The Toltec I Ching
  with Martha Ramirez-Oropeza

In the Oneness of Time: The Education of a Diviner

Way of the Diviner

When You Catch the Fish, Throw Away the Net: An Autobibliography

The Divine Dark: Mystery as Origin and Destination

In Search of the Inevitable: Signatures of Celestial Divination

The Oracle Whispers: Echoes from the Edge of Creation

RESEARCHES ON THE TOLTEC I CHING:

  Vol. 1. *I Ching Mathematics: The Science of Change*

  Vol. 2. *The Image and Number Treatise: The Oracle and the War on Fate*

  Vol. 3. *The Forest of Fire Pearls Oracle: The Medicine Warrior I Ching*

  Vol. 4. *I Ching Mathematics for the King Wen Version*

  Vol. 5. *Why Study the I Ching: A Brief Course in the Direct Seeing of Reality*

  Vol. 6. *The Open Secret I Ching: The Diviner's Journey and the Road of Freedom*

  Vol. 7. *The Alchemical I Ching: 64 Keys to the Secret of Internal Transmutation*

  Vol. 8. *intrachange: I Ching Chess*

  Vol. 9. *The Before Heaven I Ching: Reading the Text of Creation*

  Vol. 10. *I Ching Talismans: Forge of Spiritual Sigils*

SELF-REALIZATION PRACTICES:

  The Five Emanations: Aligning the Modern Mind with the Ancient Soul

  The Spiritual Basis of Good Fortune: Retracing the Ancient Path of Personal Transformation

  Facing Light: Preparing for the Moment of Dying

  The Art of Divination: The Role of Consciousness and Will in Stepping Outside Time

POETRY:

  Palimpsest Flesh

  Fragments of Anamnesia

  The Soul of Power: Deconstructing the Art of War

  The Tao of Cool: Deconstructing the Tao Te Ching

  We Are I Am: Visions of Mystical Union

NOVEL:

  Life and Death in the Hotel Bardo

Made in the USA
Middletown, DE
03 October 2023

40103678R00099